Nothing
Needs to be
the Way it's Always Been

By *Dawn C. Walton*

Copyright © 2012 by Dawn C. Walton
All rights reserved.

ISBN: 1478307684
ISBN-13: 9781478307686

Foreword

I would like to thank my husband – "The Hubby" for his unconditional love since I met him. His unerring belief in me has never failed to amaze me and I love him dearly. Most things I have achieved in my adult life are because he has always encouraged me and been there for me.

Thank you to my daughter "The little one" who was my inspiration to change and become everything I could be.

Thank you to my son, Adam, who, although no longer with us, taught me that I was capable of being a mother and loving.

Thank you to Sandra Roycroft-Davis who started me on this journey with the Thinking Slimmer product but stepped out from running a company to pick up the phone and talk to me. Her ability to care for every single person she comes across is what led me to Trevor.

And then the other main character in this book, Trevor Silvester. He is not just a therapist and not just the founder of Cognitive Hypnotherapy. I find it hard to find the words to describe what an amazing man he is. He treats each of his clients with the utmost respect as individuals rather than people with problems. He doesn't draw boundaries around his clients to keep them in boxes because he believes we all have within us whatever we need to overcome our problems. He works with his clients, not on them. Once he has taken hold of your hand to help you, he won't let go until you let go first. And even then he continues to walk alongside you so that you know with the slightest movement his hand will be there again.

Because of Trevor I was able to transform from 40 years of hating myself to being excited about my life and myself. I did this in just under a year. This book is my story.

There is a phrase: "It's never too late to have a happy childhood". It's an interesting thought. I don't agree with it in its absolute form – but I certainly believe it's never too late to let go of an unhappy childhood and have a happy life.

This book is a collection of posts from my blog. I have been blogging for many years and I use my blog as a modern journal. Unlike a traditional journal, this one is held online for all to see (and comment on). For this book I have taken all the posts that I wrote in relation to my personal journey and brought them together into one place so you can see the whole story. The nice thing about this approach is you get to join me on this journey real time – without any editing or revisions. What I felt, you get to see.

I hope enjoy sharing this journey with me.

1 - Introduction 1

2 - Session 1 7

17th June, 2011 It's a new day, it's a new Dawn.... 9

18th June, 2011 Blue skies and raindrops 11

19th June, 2011 Father's Day. .15

20th June, 2011 Positive of the day. 17

21st June, 2011 Positive of the day 19

22nd June, 2011 Positive of the day 21

23rd June, 2011 Positive of the day. 23

24th June, 2011 The week my life changed 25

28th June, 2011 Another change 29

30th June, 2011 You know best. 33

3rd July, 2011 Birthdays. 35

3rd July, 2011 Defining yourself 37

5th July 2011 Consequences .39

6th July, 2011 About today? 43

7th July, 2011 Lessons learned 47

14th July, 2011 Tony. 51

15th July, 2011 Lifetime CV. .53

18th July, 2011 Choice. 55

20th July, 2011 Operation Happiness. 57

24th July, 2011 Derailed. 61

25th July 2011 I'm an idiot 65

27th July, 2011 On the cusp .69

3 - Session 2 71

30th July, 2011 Load bearing stick 73

1st August, 2011 Stimulation 77

2nd August, 2011 Team building 81

7th August, 2011 Going nowhere 83

9th August, 2011 The power of the mind 85

12th August, 2011 A different flavour of misery 89

14th August, 2011 Screen burn-in 93

18th August, 2011 A new Dawn - A bit of a summary . . .95

24th August, 2011 Thinking Positive 101

27th August, 2011 The big switch 105

31st August, 2011 Experts and learning. 107

1st September, 2011 I want... 111

3rd September, 2011 Forgive me, I'm perfect 113

9th September, 2011 My name is Dawn and I am. 115

22nd September, 2011 Easy as 1, 2, 3 119

4 - Session 3 121

23rd September, 2011 I don't know how to write this . .123

27th September, 2011 Running reflections 125

4th October, 2011 Feel first, think later 129

18th October, 2011 Looking forward not backwards . .133

19th October, 2011 The battle of man vs food 135

25th October, 2011 I'm a baby giraffe 139

7th November, 2011 Hugs and Copying. 141

13th November, 2011 Reality and Belief. 143

17th November, 2011 World prematurity day. 147

21st November, 2011 Cognitive Hypnotherapy.
Weekend 2 of 10. 153

24th November, 2011 The Battle 157

8th December, 2011 The word "Step" 161

19th December, 2011 Thinking Slimmer 31 weeks . .167

20th December, 2011
The London Marathon and me 169

23rd December, 2011 In 2012... 173

29th December, 2011 Reflections
from 2011 into 2012 175
3rd January, 2012 On reflection 179
10th January, 2012 But now it's different 183
5 – Session 4 187
15th January, 2012 Weekend 4,
day 2 - subcon is still a git 189
18th January, 2012 Unburdened 193
23rd January, 2012 Into the wardrobe 197
2nd February, 2012 Everything changes 201
6th February, 2012 203
7th February, 2012 My brother 205
9th February, 2012 Feel the fear and do it anyway . .209
12th February, 2012 Weekend 5 - Day 2 211
14th February, 2012 Quantum leap and me 215
22nd February, 2012 I'm back 221
19th March, 2012 Getting to know me 225
27th March, 2012 Feeling pathetic 229
18th April, 2012 I don't cry .233
25th April, 2012 Virgin London Marathon 2012.
Done 235
30th April, 2012 Living in an alternate reality 247
6th May, 2012 My sister 249
9th May, 2012 Not quite there 253
6 – Session 5 255
13th May, 2012 Deep in thought 257
15th May, 2012 The Gallery - Born to Run 261
18th May, 2012 If I can do what I love I can love
who I am 265
22nd May, 2012 Ha! I ran the marathon 269

7 – The Beginning 271
      24th May, 2012 I forgive you .273
      27th May, 2012 What forgiveness means 275
      2nd June, 2012 Let me introduce you.... 279
Appendix – A comment from the hubby 283
About the author: 287

1 – Introduction

Dawn C. Walton

My whole life I have been conditioned to not talk. To not reveal the secrets of what went on at home. Keep up the front and don't ever tell. But that conditioning didn't apply to the written word and over the last few years I've discovered that I can write what I can't speak.

As I embarked on a journey to transform myself in June 2011, I found that it helped me and others to write down what was going on in my mind. This book describes that journey – a series of blog posts tracking how I transformed from a person who hated living, a person who never looked forward to the next minute let alone the next year and a person who was unable to appreciate the people and things in her life. I transformed in the space of a year into a person who loves her life, loves her friends and family, and even more importantly, loves herself.

It started on Twitter.

I read about a product call Thinking Slimmer which was basically an MP3 that you listened to every day and it reprogrammed your brain to think about food differently. I was significantly overweight and knew that if I was to lose weight permanently then I needed to do something other than dieting. This seemed to be the answer – certainly according to some of my friends on Twitter.

So I bought it and started listening. It was pleasant enough to listen to but I was starting to believe it wouldn't work for me. I had only been listening for about 4 days but I knew I had an emotional connection to food that came from my childhood. I tweeted that I didn't think it would work and was surprised

Nothing Needs to be the Way it's Always Been

when the head honcho of Thinking Slimmer, Sandra, responded with an offer of help.

The next day I spoke to Sandra on the phone and after she asked me a couple of questions she had worked out what the connection was. She told me that it probably would work but that it would be worth me seeing some bloke called Trevor Silvester. Trevor was apparently the genius behind Thinking Slimmer and the founder of a therapeutic approach called Cognitive Hypnotherapy.

Sandra didn't try and convince me to see him, but she did explain that she felt he could help me and that this would be possible in just a few sessions. Many years before I had seen a person-centred counsellor for nearly a year and a half and whilst I had seen some improvement, it wasn't permanent or fundamental enough to make a difference.

I wasn't sure.

But I really wanted to believe that there was a way out of the dark pit I lived in.

Why? Because since my daughter came into my life I wanted to make sure she had the best life possible and to do that I had to be comfortable in myself.

My daughter had started asking "are you happy, mummy?" and despite the reassurances of friends that it was just about her learning to read emotions, she seemed to be doing it so much I was beginning to think I was giving her a reason to ask.

I always answered "Yes" but I hated lying to her. It stuck in my throat when I answered.

After hearing about Trevor, I dared to start believing that one day I might be able to answer "yes" and believe it. I read his book and I asked him endless questions about it and how it applied to me before we had our first session.

Each time he answered patiently.

Dawn C. Walton

And as we approached that first session I was beginning to believe that Sandra was right. Maybe this man really could help me.

As you read this book, you will share my journey from the night before that first session, right through to the point where I was answering "Yes, I am happy" honestly to my daughter.

By the way, she never asks any more because she knows the answer will always be "Yes"!

2 – Session 1

Dawn C. Walton

17th June, 2011

It's a new day, it's a new Dawn...

I went to sleep late. Not to bed. That was fine but sleep took a lot longer.
I had many weird dreams. More than usual.
I woke up early. Way, way too early.

I am sitting here now sipping a coffee and waiting for a more appropriate time to head to the airport. It's only 10 minutes away and I'm already checked in for a flight that's not until 8:25am.

It's 6am now.

I am sipping my coffee and looking out on a gorgeous sunny, still day. Perfect flying conditions.

Spud the cat is attacking a leaf, having spent 5 minutes cuddling, kneading and purring on me.

For once I'm not travelling to London with work.

For once I'm doing something that is totally about me.

Nothing Needs to be the Way it's Always Been

Today I'm heading for the first of only a few cognitive hypnotherapy sessions.

Today I'm re-programming myself with a little help.

Today should change my life.
I've also done everything on my task list today, both personal and work wise. I am on fire!

18th June, 2011

Blue skies and raindrops

Not quite sure how to write this post. I told you yesterday about the step I was taking to change my life. I went to see a Cognitive Hypnotherapist in London.

I am going to share with you how this went but I am not going to give you too much detail because that is personal. Tricky, eh? In fairness, throughout this blog you have always been told how I'm feeling. Sometimes you've been told why, sometimes you've had hints, and sometimes it's just about feeling. This won't change.

I am not going to tell you why I went to see the Cognitive Hypnotherapist. I will, however, tell you the impact

The session was tough. I came out of it feeling exhausted and shaken and wandering around in a little bit of a daze.

I bugged out of meeting up with someone and just made my way back to the airport for my flight home in 4 hours.

I stayed in that somewhat dazed state for 4 or 5 hours. My mind processing again and again what had happened.

Nothing Needs to be the Way it's Always Been

"Don't expect this to be an instant fix" had been the warning. We had done a couple of weeks of preparation via email – so we were at least starting at a run but the process is a cumulative one, with exercises and a recording being used to constantly reinforce the initial re-programming.

By the time I boarded my flight later in the evening, I was beginning to feel lighter in myself. The exhaustion and shaking had all but gone. In fact, I was feeling almost buoyant.

I sat on my seat in the plane and waited for everyone to board.

Then I had a thought.

In my head, there was silence.

Now normally my head is filled with a voice that is constantly swearing at me and putting me in my place. Reminding me how useless I am (it's my own voice by the way). I think I have told you in a previous post how there would not be a single positive thing I could say about myself.

I sat quietly and thought. Nope it wasn't there.

So I then challenged myself. "What do you think about yourself?"

"You're ok", was the answer.

Seriously? This has NEVER happened before. It is a totally unfamiliar feeling to me. I spent the 1.5 hour flight thinking and, to be honest, waiting and dreading the voice returning. It didn't.

Dawn C. Walton

I bounced in the door to greet my hubby. He'd had a long day with the little one and I was able to genuinely feel for him rather than be caught up in myself.

This morning, I woke up. I looked for the voice. It still wasn't there.

I have spent the morning feeling like I am on drugs, I am that high! I keep grinning inanely to myself.

As I returned from Sainsbury's with the little one, I experienced a small knot in my stomach. There was no voice that went with it. I wondered – could this be what it feels like to be happy? I'm really not sure.

As the afternoon progresses I feel the edge going off my happy state. I know this could easily slip back and I will work really hard to make this a permanent change.

So one of the exercises is to note down each day every positive change or difference I notice in my behaviour. I am going to do that on this blog as I write a post every day so I may as well put it on here. This blog is ultimately for me after all, and I look forward to looking back at my journey in the future.

I think today's positive is pretty obvious.

But let's have an extra, eh? This morning I woke up to the sound of the rain beating on the window and was looking forward to getting up and seeing what I could do with the little one all day.

Dawn C. Walton

19ᵗʰ June, 2011

Father's Day

I hate Father's Day. Crappy fathers blah blah blah. Commercialisation blah blah blah.

Hubby is a brilliant dad blah blah blah.

We made him a card and also a bookmark. She's only 1 month off being 3 so I used poetic licence!

The little one and I went to McDonalds for brekkie. Tigger came too. The hubby stayed at home and had a lie-in. We don't usually take him brekkie back with us but we did today.

Tigger tried to nick my coffee. Naughty Tigger!

The little one has been asking to go to the beach all week so I took her, leaving the hubby at home to play his online game. Amazingly, it was a gorgeous day. So much so, I wish I'd packed for a day at the beach. Luckily I had suncream in the car and was able to apply it liberally.

We went to the park by the beach. Well Monkey (the one from the PGTips advert) went on all the rides. There was an incident with a younger little boy who pushed and kicked out at the little one. I know kids do these things. But the father just went over to him, picked him up, said "are you being naughty" and then "shall we go and find

Nothing Needs to be the Way it's Always Been

your brother?". He didn't have the decency to say sorry and get the boy to apologise. I stopped the little one crying by pointing out it was only the same as she did to Spud. That shut her up!

We picked up an ice cream on the way home for her and the hubby.

We went out for a walk locally and managed to find some ripe wild strawberries. When we got back home I made a roast using the pork belly recipe.

Suffice to say, the little one isn't the only knackered one today.

For me the day did not see me in the same high mood as yesterday. In fact, the opposite – I felt quite low. I heard the old voice creeping back a little but it was very quiet and far away, more a mumbling voice. I listened to the track given to me on Friday after my session this afternoon and the bad mood lifted a lot.

POSITIVE OF THE DAY NUMBER 2

The little one is an amazing child. She is frightened of nothing and no-one. She is caring and affectionate (most of the time although sometimes loses it with the kitten) and loves a cuddle. This is great because I totally love cuddling her too. She is fun and so good natured that if she's not happy you know it's because something is wrong. She copies everything we do. And that is the crux of my positive observation for the day. If she copies so much, and if she is so brilliant, then that must be in part because of me as her mother. I may not feel this deep down yet but I know that will come. Bringing these things to the front of our mind leaves it open to defining a new reality based on them. Baby steps but I WILL get there!

Dawn C. Walton

20th June, 2011

Positive of the day

I don't really have anything to blog about today, but it's important that I share with you my positives as I go through this journey for the better, happier me.

Today was a challenge as once more I woke up in a foul mood. My therapist (get me, all lah de dah) explained that as I listen to a track before bed, that reinforces what we covered, this mood is likely to be the result of all the processing that happened through the night.

But, and this is the key, it is up to us to choose our mood. So from tomorrow I shall go for a walk or a run, outside, every morning before I start work. I will start the day feeling good.I have made huuuuuuuuuuuge progress since my session on Friday. In fact, it's a bit like Thinking Slimmer (which uses the same approach, by the way) in that it is almost inconceivable that I could see this much difference in such a short space of time. I am no longer seeking answers. I don't need them. Things just were the way they were.

My new journey is about finding happiness.

Positive of the day number 3

The big positive is the lack of questions I now have about my past. I don't feel the need for answers any more. It's a totally

Nothing Needs to be the Way it's Always Been

bizarre feeling but my past is a storybook as opposed to an experience. I really feel like I am taking control of my life in a way I never have before and already I'm able to share that. Today, I was talking to a colleague who was expressing some of the frustrations he had with our boss's annoying behaviour. I managed to give him some suggestions how we could turn them into something funny and entertaining instead. He left the call with me laughing and sounding upbeat and saying "Thank you". That made me feel good.

Dawn C. Walton

21st June, 2011

Positive of the day

Today is the Summer Solstice – the longest day of the year. It is also, I am sure, the longest rainy day in history. It's bucketing down!

I, at last, managed to get on top of some of the work backlog that built up while my head was upside down the last couple of weeks and I should be able to consolidate the work before my boss returns from holiday next week and make sure he's none the wiser to my uselessness!

Other news is that the hubby's best friend is incredibly ill in intensive care right now. They gave him 24-48 hours to live yesterday. They said that if he makes it through the next 48 hours he will go into terminal care as his kidneys have totally failed and his blood is shot. He has leukacmia. He's had it for about 6 years now which, given they gave him only about a year to live, is a good run. In the last couple of weeks they put him on a new experimental drug after he'd tried everything else with no success. It seems that the drug not only didn't work but had the opposite effect and took him right down.

The hubby was faced with an impossible decision last night: to drive down to Manchester to see a good friend who is not conscious and may not gain consciousness or stay here and wait for a phone call, preserving the memory. He decided that whatever he decided, he would probably regret it but made the tough choice not to go there. His friend has a big family and lots of friends down there and the hubby didn't want to get in the way. They talk a lot anyway – there was nothing left unsaid.

So now we are just waiting for the phone call. It's a horrible situation to be in. The hubby is doing all he can to distract himself but nothing changes how hard this is.

So on that note, on to my positive of the day, and yes, despite this going on, there still is one here.

Positive of the day number 4

Yesterday it was pointed out to me that I can choose my mood. I don't have to start the day in a bad mood as my brain does its processing. So this morning I got up with a plan to go for a walk or run down the path near the house. I opened the curtains to pouring rain.

But I love the rain. I love going out and getting drenched and then coming home to a nice hot shower and clean dry clothes. So I got togged up with trainers and iPod shuffle and headed off. I ran 10 minutes down the path and walked/ran 10 minutes back. When I got home, dripping wet, I offered a big cuddle to the little one but for some reason she didn't want one!

After my shower I sat and thought "I am in a good mood". Result! The mood has stayed with me most of the day so far although I had a little dip after lunchtime.

So today's positive is that I can choose my mood and I'm choosing to be in a good mood.

22nd June, 2011

Positive of the day

I went for a run/walk again today. Again in the rain. I have been waking up in such a bad mood it's great to do something to shift it. I think I actually would prefer it to be raining. I feel so refreshed after a shower and with clean dry clothes on.

Positive of the day number 5.

When you are totally engrossed in your own misfortune and the ongoing trials of life, it is very hard to look out and see others in your world. When you connect with other people and say "I know how you're feeling" and feel that you are empathising or sympathising with them, this isn't the best thing you can do. By saying this, you are projecting your emotions on to them, you are giving your own emotions a voice and the affirmation that "everything sucks", "it's tough" etc.

I have accepted that everything doesn't suck. I am in a good mood and no longer feel the pain of past events. Because of this, for the first time I have my eyes open to really see everyone else. And to be able to connect with everyone else. Instead of looking for common ground between what they feel and what I feel, I now just ask myself "what can I do to help them?" If I can do this, in even the smallest way each day, then I feel even better about myself.

Dawn C. Walton

23rd June, 2011

Positive of the day

Oh gosh, this is getting more difficult as the days go by, isn't it? Sometimes the changes are so small that it makes it hard to notice. It's just a little shift in perception. This happened in a conversation I had yesterday. Someone pointed out to me that if I couldn't help someone that it wasn't a reflection on me. "I know", I answered. And it's true.

After 4 really early morning starts (with yesterday's being 5:30am!!) the hubby said he would take the night shift and hence the early start. Now go on, guess what time the little one was up? 7am. Were you close? You see 7am, is the time the Gro Clock is set to show the sun – a sign it is OK to get up. She bounded through happily "Hello daddy, I slept through and I waited till the sun came up".

Now guess what time my stupid brain woke me up. 6am. Honestly! How annoying. If it was my body waking me up, I could have gone back to sleep but it was my brain so I was scuppered. I decided to get up and tidy the lounge, quietly. Rock and roll!

So inevitably, despite my hubby's efforts, I am still knackered today. Keeping positive and upbeat is very hard when you are tired. I may not be very buoyant but neither am I feeling low! So ha! World, that's you told…

Nothing Needs to be the Way it's Always Been

Positive of the day number 6

So here is what I have realised. My help being rejected by a friend is nothing to do with me. It is not a reflection of who I am. It does not mean I am a bad and horrible person. The issue actually sits with the friend. This may seem like quite a minor statement to you but to me, accepting this is a big deal. When you feel you are useless, you very much need external validation to make you feel good about yourself and value yourself. When that is rejected it's easy to go into a spiral of self-loathing. When you accept that you are actually OK, that people are friends with you, not for what you can do for them, but for who you fundamentally are, then you can also accept that sometimes they may not want your help. You can accept that this is OK.

Dawn C. Walton

24th June, 2011

The week my life changed

When I wrote my post "It's a new day, it's a new Dawn" a week ago, I dared to hope that meeting Trevor for a session of Cognitive Hypnotherapy would change my life.

We had been communicating via email since I first booked the session so had a pretty good understanding of what to expect from each other.

I dared to hope because I'd been doing Thinking Slimmer for 6 weeks with great success (it is Trevor who is the brains and the voice behind the track that so many of us now listen to). I knew that the way he works is really effective. I knew it worked for me. What I didn't know, and wasn't sure of, was if it would work for everything about me. For all my problems.

I dared to hope that I could look at myself in the mirror without wanting to run away. I dared to hope that I could be a more positive and happy person for my family.

I didn't, for one moment, imagine that my hopes would be well founded and that my life would actually change. I didn't expect the changes to start impacting that same day. I couldn't have possibly imagined how much of a

Nothing Needs to be the Way it's Always Been

different person I feel today from the person I was only 1 week ago.

In just over an hour, Trevor was able to challenge all the fundamental beliefs I held about myself in such a way that it worked at the core of my thinking. In such a way that my brain could accept it. In such a way that didn't involve huge emotional upheaval. Don't get me wrong, there is nothing about my session that I could call fun. I came out of it shaken and exhausted. But it was a constructive session. I felt shaken for a reason other than having raked up a bunch of painful memories.

If you follow this blog you will have joined me on my journey since my session. I know, because a few of you have commented, that the change in me is tangible even through the written word alone. You will have seen the positive of the day that I have posted each day. I will post one with this post but I think I may be struggling to do one daily from now on. So many big changes!

Our session is reinforced by a track that Trevor recorded at the end that I now listen to every night. That is further reinforced by me focussing on the positives I see each day (hence the positive of the day) which brings the right thinking to the front of my mind, making it more open to the track.

I have another session booked for the end of July (Trevor is, as you would expect, a very busy guy!) but my progress is beyond comprehension. Even more so considering I had only 1 session of Cognitive Hypnotherapy. We have more to do. Trevor continues to be hugely supportive on email and patiently answers

Dawn C. Walton

my questions and helps me overcome my wobbles. But even if it all stopped where it is right now – it has been brilliant.

Positive of the day number 7

This one is gonna be a doozy – are you ready?

1. *I told you before that there wasn't a single thing I liked about myself. I don't feel like that any more. I am comfortable with who I am. I accept I have strengths (although a bit much for me to be able to state them yet!). I accept that I am neither unlikable nor unlovable. My hubby and the little one love me. I accept that now.*

2. *I do feel emotions. Do you think that's a weird thing to say? I don't. For me, emotions have always felt like dangerous territory. I have felt, if I exposed myself to really feeling anything I would lose all control and lose my mind. I can love and laugh and cry and that is all part of normal life. And one day, I will write down "I am happy" and I will mean it and I will experience it in all its glory. It is safe to feel.*

3. *There is only 1 Dawn. There is no such thing as the one that you all see and the "real" me. They are one and the same. It is OK to accept that when I do something well, that it is really me. Right down to the core. There are many things I do well.*

Dawn C. Walton

28th June, 2011

Another change

This post contains details about the loss of a baby. Please don't read if this will distress you.

You are all well used to me banging on about Adam at this time of year.

This is a slightly different post.

This is a post that comes from the life-changing journey I am on right now.

It seems, once more, I underestimated Trevor.

You may have read how my life changed in the space of a week? Well, the repercussions of that were wider than I expected.

The other day I was struggling. Quite a lot. I was watching my hubby suffer as he worried about his dying friend. As he battled with himself over what was the right thing to do, go down and see him or stay here and preserve the memories. We were in that situation where we were waiting for a phone call to tell us someone we cared for had died – just like it was with Adam.

As everything started getting on top of me, I mailed Trevor, concerned I was slipping back and losing all my positive progress.

Nothing Needs to be the Way it's Always Been

Trevor mailed back quickly and not only gave me a little nudge back on track but also opened my eyes to another lesson. A lesson I am going to share with you now just in case it makes as much sense to you as it did to me.

Positive of the day number 8

It is not necessary to feel pain to remember someone who died. The memory comes from the love you felt.

Adam was my first child. Because of the circumstances, when he was born he was taken away to Neonatal Intensive Care Unit. Because of the timing, after an hour or so the hubby got kicked out and had to go home. Here I am, in hospital, recovering from a C-section having delivered at bang on 26 weeks pregnant. I don't have my baby and I don't have my hubby.

The hubby was back first thing and went to see him. He came through to tell me all about him. I had a picture and was trying to express so that Adam had every chance to survive. But I had no connection. Nothing. I hadn't carried him to term, and because of the problems he wasn't a very mobile bump.

As soon as it was practical I forced myself to go and see him. Yes, that's right. There was no instinct making me go. But I did. From that point forward I went 3 times a day to spend an hour or 2 with him. I eventually took Harry Potter in to read to him so that he could constantly hear my voice while I was there (totally screwed up my enjoyment of the first Harry Potter book!). I took pictures and videos. Still can't watch the video,s of course!

In 4 weeks I held him twice. And then he was cabled up.

I never got flesh contact. I never got to cuddle him. The first night the hubby slept in the hospital with me because they

Dawn C. Walton

thought he was going to die. Every day after it looked like he was going to die. It tore us both apart. We operated on hope and let the doctors do the medical bit. We said we would make all decisions in his interest and never let him suffer, even if it meant we would.

The key decision came after 4 weeks. I've written all about it before and I'm not going to share again. Suffice to say it marked the end. After a tear developed in his stomach lining he was now suffering and after dosing him up on morphine we switched his incubator off. We held our breath and hoped he would breathe. He didn't and that was probably a really good thing. But as he died, so did that last bit of hope. This was the only time I cuddled him and I really wish I had held him closer.

How can this possibly be under the positive of the day?

I have carried the pain of losing Adam for 4 years now. The pain was necessary to make me feel. I have avoided "feeling" for so long to protect myself. In fairness, that's probably all that got me through the time with Adam.

Each year I feel the pain of his death to remind myself that I loved him. Because I was never sure if I did. I was never sure if I had the connection. I used it as a weapon on myself – jabbing myself and hurting each time.

But I know now that I did love him. With all my heart. In the same way as I love the hubby and I love the little one. I loved Adam. You have no idea what a relief it is for me to realise that. To accept that. I don't have to feel pain to feel. Of course I would have loved to bring him home and have a life with him like we have with the little one. But it was not to be.

I love you Adam. I'm still sorry. But I want you to know that I love you.

Dawn C. Walton

30th June, 2011

You know best

It's definitely an interesting journey I am on right now.

I am discovering different shades of feeling and therefore different moods that go with that. It has been a little disturbing, in all honesty. I pride myself on being in control, on taking everything in my stride and letting nothing affect me.

I have to analyse and understand every change in my mood. I attach huge amounts of meaning to even the smallest moments. In the Thinking Slimmer Slimpod (the track that you listen to daily) it talks about trusting your subconscious to do what is best for you but that is a really hard thing to do.

Each day seems to be a battle between the subconscious and conscious. The concept of letting go, surfing the wave of day-to-day feelings and not attaching any hidden meaning is a little alien. Why do I feel like this? Am I slipping back and losing my positive outlook? What are the wider implications of feeling like this?

Just being who I am remains a challenge.

Just accepting the dimensions of "me", even more so.

Nothing Needs to be the Way it's Always Been

Every change in mood currently causes me to evaluate who I am and I need to move away from this.

Positive of the day number 9

Sometimes you are just in a bad mood. In the same way you are in a great mood sometimes. It doesn't mean anything.

When you are in a good mood, do you question it? Do you wonder what it is about you that puts you in a good mood? Do you try and establish some hidden meaning in your past that led you to it? Probably not.

So why does it always have to be that way with a bad mood? It doesn't have any deep and hidden meaning. It's just a mood and it will pass. You may be able to drive the mood away (fresh air, dancing to loud music, a nice cup of coffee, read a book) but sometimes it will pass on its own. Don't look for meaning where none may exist.

Dawn C. Walton

3rd July, 2011

Birthdays

On July 3rd 2007 I had planned to go to a lovely steakhouse-style restaurant in St Andrews called Ziggy's for dinner with my hubby and best friend to celebrate the birthday they shared.

Instead I was in hospital overnight, pregnant with Adam, with my blood pressure too high and concerns from his scan.

I asked the hubby and friend to go anyway. Obviously they didn't.

3 days later, after another scan they told me we would have to deliver because they were concerned about blood flow to him. That afternoon he was delivered at 1lb 6oz by emergency C-section. The rest is history.

For the next couple of years we didn't celebrate the hubby's birthday.

Last year we realised it didn't make things any easier to ignore it. We may as well get something out of the day.

So now we celebrate. But nothing changes the fact that the day has so much meaning. I am lower right now than I've been in a long time.

It will pass.

Nothing Needs to be the Way it's Always Been

I no longer attach any wider significance or deeper meaning to the way it makes me feel. This is progress. But the feelings remain.

So today the hubby got an amazing Dell Alienware gaming PC as his pressie. He is very happy. It also came in some great packaging that the little one loved to play with.

Soon it will be the little one's bedtime and I will collapse for a while. I just need to ride these next few weeks and make sure I don't attach any greater to significance to them than "Adam died and that sucks".

3rd July, 2011

Defining yourself

It's 2 weeks since my Cognitive Hypnotherapy session with Trevor. You know, the one that changed my life?

I continue to listen to my track that he recorded for me every night and although it's not a daily occurrence, I continue to reframe my beliefs about my past and who I am under Trevor's patient guidance.

The last 3 or 4 days I have had a raging torrent of nervous energy coursing through me. It feels like I am hugely nervous about something. But I'm not.

On reflection, I have come to the conclusion it is anger. I think, as the other feelings I have about my past get negated, I am left with a feeling of anger over what happened. Borderline rage. Now this is something that I am not used to experiencing. Anger has always been a big no-no for me and one of the reasons that it may feel like I'm about to explode is that I don't really know what to do with it.

As a result I am impatient, tetchy and not at my happiest, for sure. I then get scared. I feel like I am demonstrating behaviours that I myself am really scared of and that I am going to scare the little one. I feel like I'm turning

Nothing Needs to be the Way it's Always Been

into the wicked White Witch from Narnia. I can see myself as her really clearly.

Another re-focussing was needed. Trevor pointed me at the little one. If I was that bad, would the little one really be so happy and balanced? Would she laugh at me when I'm cross with her? Giggle in my face when I shout at her? If I am, in fact, the wicked White Witch wouldn't you be able to see that in the little one?

Even I can see that isn't the case. As I write this she has just come up to me, given me a gold star sticker and told me it is because "You are such a good mummy".

Meanwhile I need to release this angry energy. I feel like I need to go into the middle of a field and have a total and utter meltdown. It may dissipate on its own but right now it just keeps building.

Positive of the day number 10

You only need to replicate the behaviour of the people who brought you up if you choose to. You are truly your own person with your own characteristics and a unique set of values.

How you to choose to live your life, be a mother and partner or behave in any relationship is down to no-one other than yourself. It is a choice and not pre-determined path based on your experiences.

Dawn C. Walton

5th July 2011

Consequences

So here is a bit of advice. Do not go to a life-changing Cognitive Hypnotherapy session that starts to teach you to listen and tap into your emotions for the first time in your life 2 weeks before the anniversary of just about the most emotionally distressing thing that has ever happened in your life.

It's not going to end well.

Tomorrow would have been Adam's 4th Birthday.

2 weeks ago, Trevor helped me connect with myself enough to realise that I did, in fact, love Adam, where I had doubted I could really love anyone before.

So this year, as I approach the anniversary of his birth I have found myself absolutely flooded with emotion. In previous years it has always been hard but I could survive it all and make it through. I welcomed the pain I felt to keep his memory alive. This year I have been overwhelmed by the emotion of losing him. Beyond anything I have been able to deal with. I would also normally take a day or two off work but critical meetings have been arranged this week that I can't get out of. I am in Newcastle in meetings for the next 2 days.

Nothing Needs to be the Way it's Always Been

This morning I woke up at 4:30am with the now-familiar nervous energy running through me. At 5am I got up and went for a run, hoping to run it off. If anything, I felt worse when I got back. I sat down and wrote the rest of the presentation that I had to deliver today. The result of 4 weeks of work. 4 weeks where I was turning everything that I had based myself on upside down.

I started to fall to pieces. I lay on my bed after my shower, listening to my Slimpod and sobbing – not understanding why.

I came downstairs and felt so unbelievably overwhelmed that I had to cancel my first call of the day. Unlike before, I have not been able to tame this emotion. To just carry on as I've always done.

Luckily I had arranged to talk to Trevor on Skype today, as this has been building up for a few days now.

I clung on to that call. I just needed to keep going until then because I knew he could help. It was hard. And it was hard because, for the first time since Adam was born and died, I was mourning his loss from a basis of love. I was feeling the pain of losing my little boy who I loved.

And then I spoke to Trevor. And he calmly and patiently helped me understand that it was OK to feel like this. That I will always feel like this. But he also helped me understand that it doesn't have to be all or nothing – meltdown or shutdown, that there are shades of emotion in between that can be managed.

Dawn C. Walton

Then he explained how I could gain some control and soften the emotion so that I can deal with it. He immediately recorded a track for me to listen to that I could apply before my critical presentation at 3pm – just 1 hour after we were talking.

Between our conversation, and the track, I regained control. I was no longer in meltdown. I am still hurting, but that's because I loved Adam and will always hurt. But I am also coping with it.

My presentation could not have gone better. In fact, one of the stakeholders I was presenting to even mailed me to thank me for the work afterwards. He just emailed me so he wasn't trying to look good (a common problem in my company).

I am exhausted now. I think the last time I had such a tough time was 4 years ago – when Adam was born. But I am also elated in a strange way. I came through it. I have learnt something more and I can keep moving forward.

Dawn C. Walton

6th July, 2011

About today?

This space is my online diary so I am going to sum up how today went so I can look back in a year's time and smile at how far I have come from this moment. Apologies for it being a bit of a moider and a bit emotional.

Today is Adam's 4th birthday and I am in a 2-day meeting in Newcastle.

I shouldn't have come. I thought I could cope because I always have before. I was wrong.

The drive down was in rain and fog. I was practising the techniques given to me by Trevor but not feeling in control. I listened to the recording he made for me before I went in to my meeting.

The first meeting was a challenge. It's almost impossible to deal with frustration when when you're feeling emotionally fragile

It kept getting worse. I was breathing and using the technique Trevor gave me but I couldn't stay in control. Tears were starting to form as discussions became heated. Breathe Dawn, breathe. I tweeted, as much for distraction as anything else. You were there and listening and supporting. Then Trevor started tweeting little

Nothing Needs to be the Way it's Always Been

techniques and words of encouragement. A little angel sat on my shoulder.

I grasped on to everything that was helping me stay in control but it was barely working.

The meeting ended just as the next one was due to start. I grabbed my phone and my keys. I walked calmly to my car and lost it. Totally and utterly lost it. I sobbed in my car with heavy rain and thunder mirroring my feelings.

I had failed. I had lost control. I spent an hour sobbing. Sobbing for Adam.

And then I worked on regaining control. Still the supportive tweets were there from Trevor and my hubby. I considered waiting until the end of the meeting at 4 and driving home. But I felt it was like getting back on the horse. If I didn't go back then, I wasn't sure I would be able to at all. So I grabbed my keys and walked slowly back to the meeting. I took a deep breath and stepped in.

I managed to make it through. I was shaking like a leaf. I was breathing. I was contributing. I was planning tomorrow.

Tomorrow morning is a team meeting and the afternoon is another performance session. I decided to try and attend the morning but to definitely not do the afternoon. My boss wasn't happy when I told him but it's tough because I can't handle that. He's lucky I will be there in the morning!

I took everyone back to the hotel at the end of the day and had a quick call with the hubby and the little one. The hubby had tripped on one of her toys, banged his

Dawn C. Walton

head on her small trampoline and knocked himself unconscious. Yes really. It's always worrying when I come away but oh em geeee!

Apparently he is OK. Oh and his best friend? The one that's dying? He's home and they had a lovely chat! How is that even possible?

Anyway I then headed off to the Metro centre to meet a friend off Twitter. I planned on shopping but the meeting had overrun so by the time I found the Starbucks it was 7pm, the time we had arranged to meet.

For 2 hours we sat and chatted over a coffee, not noticing the time going by. We avoided talking about Adam, which was good. We talked about our kids and our work and blogging and everything, actually. For 2 lovely hours I could just be me again. I found an oasis away from the shakiness and the tears and it was just what I needed. So thank you lovely Twitter pal!

So tomorrow I will attend the meeting in the morning and hopefully will cope better than I did today. And then I will go home and cuddle my hubby and the little one. Lots.

And when I get to the weekend, then maybe, at that point I will be able to look back and reflect on the lessons from this week. Maybe then I won't feel like such a failure for losing control. Maybe then I will be able to return to looking at the positives again. Maybe.

Dawn C. Walton

7th July, 2011

Lessons learned

You may have noticed that it has not been the easiest couple of days.

I'm home now. I attended the morning meeting and left before the afternoon one started. This was a very hard thing for me to do. For me it felt like failure to have to accept that due to my mental state I couldn't do some of my work.

Not only that, but it involved telling my boss I couldn't. Beyond admitting to myself I couldn't cope, I had to open up a little bit of me to tell my boss I couldn't make a meeting I was down there to attend.

This is not about him. It would have made no difference to me if he was a great boss. For me to share what had happened and the impact it was having on me is actually unprecedented.

Even here, in the relative safety of semi-anonymity of this blog (friends and family read it and know it's me) I share very few of the facts of my situation, of what caused me to embark on this journey with Trevor. You know the impact it has on me, how it makes me feel (in great detail!), but you don't know why I'm doing it and why it's working. Nor will you

Nothing Needs to be the Way it's Always Been

This morning, as I waited to take everyone to the office, I sat in my hotel room and sobbed once more. I had been shaking since I got up. I sat sobbing on my bed, looking at my watch as the minutes ticked closer to 8am when we would meet up in the lobby. "How can I do this? How can I attend the meeting today?" and then "How can I not attend it? I am committed now"

And so with a deep breath I did what I do and met everyone. They didn't notice.

We all settled down to the meeting. I was still shaking. The techniques from Trevor were no longer working for me and my head was full of thoughts about how I couldn't do this. But I worked hard to change my thinking. To adapt the techniques. To take control back and then, in a moment, it clicked into place. I found the key (with help and support again) and I was good to go. I felt a rush of adrenaline as I realised I had moved on from meltdown territory and was back to coping.

The meeting went well. I got lots of kudos for the work I'd done over the last 4 weeks leading up to the presentation I did on Tuesday. The presentation that Trevor made sure I was in a fit state to do. I showed myself that despite everything, I could still do a good job. Unconscious competence is the term, I believe.

As the meeting drew to a close the shaking returned. Probably because I was testing myself. Could I make the afternoon session? Most definitely not.

It was with a huge outpouring of relief that I tearfully sat in my car and prepared for the drive home. I had, for only the second time in my life, walked out on a meeting

Dawn C. Walton

because I was in no fit state to do it (ironically, the first time was when I attended a conference 2 months after Adam died and a breakout group was discussing "The moment that made you happiest". The first answer that someone gave was "the birth of my kids". I had to leave!)

As I drove I processed. I knew this was a learning opportunity and I didn't want to reach home having talked myself into a dark and negative place. On the other hand, I had failed to function in work and that, for me, has always been my anchor. No matter what happens, no matter how crap I feel I am, I am good at what I do.

So I processed. And I realised

I should never have gone down to the meeting in the first place. I have been experiencing the grief of losing Adam in all its rawness for the first time since he died. This was clear on Tuesday. I needed to be at home.

I did not fail. As Trevor says "Anything more than nothing is something" and I attended 2 meetings and contributed to them. I also completed on a key project despite 4 weeks of being significantly off form (in fact 2 of the 4 weeks, as I was waiting for my first session with Trevor I did nothing!).

I am not strong. I am not brave. But that is OK. Sometimes I have to say "I can't cope" or "I need help". I have never said these things before. Sometimes I should consider not toughing it out. I don't have to hide everything and pretend nothing is wrong. I can share or at least give people a heads up.

Nothing Needs to be the Way it's Always Been

The world did not stop spinning just because I stepped away for a moment. Nobody's life was dependent on my work.

So there is more to learn. I have put this post along with my others under the "Positive of the day" category because despite what I can only describe as a horrendous couple of days, I have learnt some valuable lessons.

I have also learnt what a lucky person I am to have the support of Twitter, my blog readers, friends, the hubby and Trevor. For someone who continues to feel they are worth so little, it constantly amazes me to feel the warmth of all this support.

Dawn C. Walton

14th July, 2011

Tony

Today, at 11:20am, they hubby's best friend, Tony died after battling Leukaemia.

He died peacefully in his home with friends and family around him.

I am not going to say much here. He was a lovely guy but I didn't know him for anywhere near as long as my hubby so it's not my place to write about him.

But it is a significant moment in our lives and I wanted to have it recorded on my blog. He will leave a huge hole in my hubby's life.

RIP Tony – we will all miss you.

Dawn C. Walton

15th July, 2011

Lifetime CV

I believe we all carry a "Lifetime CV" in our heads.

Like a CV we use for work, it details our experiences from the first point we remember them in chronological order.

Like a CV, it lists our experiences as a story with key events and achievements summarised succinctly.

Like a CV, those events and experiences are often packaged and modified to represent what we want to show, as opposed to the absolute facts.

We use this CV to define ourselves. When we come across a situation in our lives we need to "handle" we refer to our CVs to interpret how to respond. We communicate these CVs to those around us and expect them to interact with us on the basis of the qualities we have listed on there.

We define ourselves by them.

But a CV can and should be re-written countless times as our life changes.

And sometimes, we're not so good at writing CVs. We get it wrong when we describe some particular event. We mis-sell ourselves.

Nothing **Needs to be the Way it's Always Been**

Positive of the day number 11

Ask yourself "Who would I be if…" and think about how you would choose to define yourself if you weren't tied in to your Lifetime CV. If you re-packaged those events to have no meaning or a different meaning.

Who would I be if…

I have already discovered that, at the first level, having turned my CV into a story instead of a pot of emotions, that I am answering this question very differently. I am already someone who is not constantly looking for everything as an excuse to beat myself up. I am not a person who needs to take everything as proof of how useless I am. I am not a person who is unlikable or unlovable.

I honestly still don't know the answer to "who would I be if…".

So far I have been able to say who I am not. My lifetime CV is now only a collection of dates and events. I haven't yet written the text around who that makes me. This is the journey I am on.

Dawn C. Walton

18th July, 2011

Choice

I've been struggling for the last few days. You see, it appears, for whatever reason, our brains are more comfortable with the familiar. This is all well and good, but when the familiar is that feeling of misery, it is easy to find ourselves clinging to it even though logically we would love to move on and be happy.

Like with me.

After my first session with Trevor I found the familiar and somewhat comforting misery which had occupied my mind for over 20 years no longer had much of a foundation. Most of what I believed about myself had the rug pulled out from under it.

What remains?

What remains is a big empty space that needs filling with something else.

Now here's the catch - if you leave it empty it just refills with the familiar negative thoughts.

Even though I know it's wrong, I have been tending back towards these thoughts. Finding every excuse to beat myself up instead of looking for opportunities to fill that empty space with something new because that is a risk

Nothing Needs to be the Way it's Always Been

and it's hard. It makes me vulnerable to do something I don't know how to do.

Positive of the day number 12

One of my previous positives was about the way we can choose our mood. This positive is the next level of that. Each day we can choose to be whoever we want to be.

So we can choose to be a person who dwells on the negative and basks in our brains' chemical addiction to the reassuring familiarity of our miserable thoughts.

Or we can choose to take a deep breath, and retrain our brains. To retrain them to focus on the chemical reaction we get from the love and connection we have with the people around us. To the people who make us laugh and grin. To those people and things that make us feel good about ourselves.

Each day, we can choose to focus on feeding bacon titbits to the happy chemical bugs who live in our brains, instead of the negative chemical bugs that are vying for the same space.

You know, it's like when you go and feed some bread to the ducks, there are always some that grab it all and some that hang back. My negative bugs are very keen to grab all those bacon bits, and I have to be aware of that, and make an effort to feed the happy ones at the back.

It's not about choosing your personality – it's about how you choose to interpret the timeline of your day. How you translate that into how you feel. You can focus on the happy positive bugs, or the negative misery bugs and it really is your choice because we all have opportunities in our days and indeed our lives to pick out either and nurture them.

20th July, 2011

Operation Happiness

Secondary Title: Positive of the day number 13!

I blogged about how we need to make the choice to be happy. That we need to override our natural tendency to feed all those negative bugs and make a special effort to reach the positive ones hiding at the back. So I wanted to share with you how I was doing (and a little about my time off!).

1. A brilliant way to start the campaign is to have a couple of weeks off work. This is even more true if you've been having a little bit of a rough ride and your job is a bit pants. Those both being true – I got an immediate boost to my positive bugs by just not having to "go to work" on Monday (I work from home so it is a bit weird).

2. Work through your list. I have sorted the satnav for the car. I've sorted the vets…and a bunch of other things that I can't even remember.

3. Spend some time reconnecting/connecting with friends. I've spent some really good time with my best friend. The other evening we stayed up until 1:30am chatting and it was brilliant (even though the little

Nothing Needs to be the Way it's Always Been

one still had me up at 6:45am!). Then yesterday we went to Costco. My first trip in 3+ months. My friend came with me and it was great to hang out.

4. Have some clear goals. It's the little one's birthday on Friday and I had a Gruffalo cake to make. I've only just started but we're on the way.

5. We are going swimming tomorrow and have been out and about each day.

6. Appreciate the ones you love. The little one has had me in stitches for days. I just can't stop laughing at her, she's so funny. When we go out in the car she loves to have "Stop" by Sam Brown playing pretty much on repeat. She knows the words so well by now that she can sing without the music. So when all of us headed to Starbucks this morning she sang away to the hubby. She also sang her way around town. It was hysterical.

7. Achieve something. My weight loss continues to go well thanks to ThinkingSlimmer. Yesterday I bought 2 new pairs of 3/4 length running trousers from Costco. I bought Large instead of XL as I know I've lost weight. When I put one of them on this morning and headed out for my run (they were the tightest of the two by the way) I had to turn back because they fell down. I turned back, changed and headed out again. I ran the furthest distance yet at the fastest pace today.

So all in all I'm doing well. I've had a few days where I've worked really hard on focussing on the positives

Dawn C. Walton

and putting the negatives to one side. The old me would have taken the following to dictate my days:

1. We've had to compromise on the car and get a satnav device rather than a new car.

2. There are still size 18 trousers that don't fit due to the cut and my huge whale-like stomach. I have tonnes of weight still to lose.

3. My hubby isn't on form due to what we think is yet another infection after a scratch on his leg. He also slipped on the little one's badly placed toy in the kitchen yesterday and was in considerable pain all day

4. My filling fell out. It meant another trip to the dentist.

5. The vet won't give Spud the chop until he's 6 months and Cats Protection are already nagging. It means longer inside for him and continued cat litter.

6. There are still things that I struggle to cope with. I have many negative thoughts and have had quite a few bad dreams lately. This is not unusual for me but is something that I know will go away. I can "sink" very easily when anything doesn't go quite right and if you consider for every high there is a low, increasing my highs also increases my lows.

But…

…I haven't let those mean old Negative bugs have their way and scoff all the bacon. I've focussed on lobbing it way back there to the Positive dudes. And you know what? They are starting to come to the front on their

Nothing Needs to be the Way it's Always Been

own now. There is not enough room for them both so I think I might actually be cracking this.

So here's the thing. Yes, there have been times over the last few days where I can honestly say I have felt happy. There, I said it. Looks like the world didn't end!

Keep watching this space…

Dawn C. Walton

24th July, 2011

Derailed

I have had to press the pause button on my journey right now.

There have been a couple of things over the last few days that have derailed me. Not only has it meant that I've struggled to find any positives but I've also found myself slipping back into the old familiar cycle of negative thoughts reinforcing themselves and driving me down the age-old path of self-doubt etc.

Damn those negative bugs stealing all the bacon!

Now, let's for a moment just focus on a couple of positives (I know, I said I couldn't!).

1. The reason I have become so severely derailed is because I was on a track in the first place. Before 5 weeks ago I wasn't even on a track, I was already down the side of the bank in the undergrowth (taking the analogy too far?). I can recognise how far I have come enough to recognise I'm not there anymore.

2. I did, for a short while, think of giving up. I thought of cancelling my session on Friday. I thought I was a lost cause. See, told you I'd lost it! That is the stupidest idea. Irrespective of how I feel right now,

Nothing Needs to be the Way it's Always Been

last week was nothing short of awesome. I was HAPPY. Seriously, genuinely happy. Never in my life have I felt like that before. I reconnected with my best friend and it felt so good and made me feel good about myself. I enjoyed just being me and spending time with the hubby and the little one. I enjoyed loving them. Again, never felt like that before.

Despite the way I feel right now, there is no way I've gone back before those milestones, before 5 weeks ago when I had my first session with Trevor.

The only catch is, while I know that, I don't feel it. I am battling to get myself back up the bank to the track. I can see it. I just can't get a grip on the scree and keep sliding back.

Meanwhile, Trevor had recorded me a new track which totally removed that anxiety I had been feeling so much a couple of weeks ago. Unfortunately that feeling is now back. It's a different source and more like feeling tense than anxious. Net effect is the same, though. I am shaky and have a stupidly short fuse. I can't take anything going wrong without wanting to burst into tears (I mean even knocking a can of Coke over!) Quite frankly, it's ridiculous.

I don't think I'm going to be able to do this one on my own. It's a good job I'm seeing Trevor on Friday and it's a really good job I'm off work again this week.

So I have to apologise because it is unlikely that I'll be sharing any lessons learned on this blog this week. I will also avoid, where possible, letting this darker

Dawn C. Walton

place I'm sitting in seep through to my tweets. It is temporary.

So here I am again, once more counting down the days to my next session on Friday and quite rightly expecting miracles again. By Saturday I will be back on track to Amazingville!

Dawn C. Walton

25th July 2011

I'm an idiot

No news there, eh?

But I really am.

Why?

Well, there has been so much going on the last 5 weeks, hasn't there? I've brought you along on the journey with me. You've seen how things have gradually got better and better.

You've seen the meltdown I had over Adam's birthday.

You've seen that I found out what it's like to feel happy and how I learnt to really love those around me and appreciate that they love me.

You've learnt about positive and negative bugs, choosing your mood and making choices on our lifetime CV.

Recently, you have seen how I've become a little derailed by a couple of things. How I almost felt like giving up – but didn't.

Last night I went to bed and found myself lying there sobbing. Proper, full on, tears-streaming-down-my-face sobbing.

Nothing Needs to be the Way it's Always Been

And I thought to myself "hang on a second, this isn't the sort of reaction I would expect for any of the things that derailed me. This is something else".

And that's when I realised. I'm an idiot.

You see, Adam was born on the 6th July, 2007.

He died on the 5th August, 2007.

That's right. This time, that year he was still alive.

In fact, at this time we were daring to believe he might come home with us. On one particular morning after an early visit where he'd had a good night, we went and picked up breakfast from McDonalds and sat in the park and talked about our future together as a family.

And so as I lay there and sobbed I realised that I am still grieving. I got so caught up in everything else. I was so happy to somehow survive a working week with his birthday in it that I failed to acknowledge that this was never about 1 day. This is about a month. A month where we suffered the tortures of the damned from minute to minute as we waited for a phone call to tell us he was going to die. A phone call that did eventually come.

Oh and of course, just over a week ago my hubby's best friend died. Another phone call that we were waiting on. Another loss making this time of year so bad.

And in the middle of it? Birthdays. The little ones and the hubby's. The opposite end of the spectrum to the deaths. I wondered why I didn't delight as much in the little one's birthday as I should have done.

Dawn C. Walton

Because, unfortunately, it will always be tinged with sadness.

So you see, I'm an idiot. Sometimes I am just too stupid to see what is right in front of my nose.

Oh and it's OK. I listened to the special track that Trevor recorded for me to calm me and help me cope around Adam's birthday a few times and I got back in control. A bit anyway.

I will get there. For the first time in a few days I have been able to look forward instead of at the ground today. I have started thinking about how I make it back to the track.

Dawn C. Walton

27th July, 2011

On the cusp

On Friday, after a gap of 6 weeks, I have session number 2 with Trevor in London. When I blogged about what was happening, I never dreamed it would be this successful. We've continued to build on this success for the last 6 weeks and there have been some real highs and successes along with some real challenges. But I am changing 20 years of programming here and it is not easy.

Imagine, if you will, a game of Kerplunk. If you remember, the object of the game is to remove sticks in turn and try and avoid releasing marbles into your tray. The one with the most marbles at the end of the game loses.

Now reverse this. The aim of the game that I'm playing with my life right now is to find the stick that releases the most marbles. It's like the marbles are my past and my memories, and the sticks are me carrying the weight of them. If I can release some of the weight I become unburdened and can move on.

As you know, there are always a couple of sticks that release a flood of marbles. In my first session with Trevor (nearly 6 weeks ago now) he found one such stick and removed it. He calls these "Significant Emotional Events"

Nothing Needs to be the Way it's Always Been

and finding the right one and the earliest possible one is critical as with one tweak you can neutralise or negate a whole bunch of negative beliefs that you have used to build your idea of self throughout your life. 1 stick, many marbles.

It was a massive change for me.

But there are still more marbles to release and more sticks to pull. We have communicated a lot over the last 6 weeks. I have kept Trevor constantly (like really, like all the time – the poor man) informed of the changes and the progress. I have pestered him with endless questions. I have doubted and celebrated.

And now I am on the cusp of session number 2. On Friday I will once again have a session with Trevor. From all our communication, I think he has a pretty good idea of which stick to pull next and if not, he knows how to work out which will be the right one.

I am terrified and emotionally exhausted. At this point, everything seems too much for me. But at the same time I am excited. Because I know how much my world changed after that first session and I am daring to dream about how amazing I will feel after this next session.

3 – Session 2

30th July, 2011

Load bearing stick

So with 24 hours to think about it and try and process what happened in my session with Trevor yesterday, it is clear that the stick we removed was a very significant one. Most, if not all, of the remaining marbles have now dropped through (read previous posts for Kerplunk reference).

This, however, has consequences that you might not have imagined.

To explain.

We took a different approach this time than in session 1. Unlike the Significant Emotional Event that Trevor dug out and used in session 1, this memory was something I was very aware of. You might even call it a traumatic memory. As such, it spent its life safely locked away and I spent my life doing my best to go nowhere near it.

Think of it as a video clip.

Now this video clip, although safely locked away in the archives, was at such an early stage in the film reel of my life, and was such a key scene to explain the plot, that despite being locked away it played a massive role in my perception of who I am and how I interact with the world.

Nothing Needs to be the Way it's Always Been

I was, of course, aware of it. I knew exactly where it was stored so I could avoid it at all costs.

The first step in rewriting this video clip was to fetch it from the archives and play it back *gulp*.

One of the things I love about Trevor's approach is you don't have to go through every painful memory and talk about it ad infinitum or analyse it. In the case of this video clip, I didn't need to tell Trevor anything about it (not that I could have) but I did need to feel it and live it so we could work on it *gulp again*. Did you realise that every time you recall a memory you change it based on your current perceptions before it gets stored again?

So that's what happened. I sat with it. Even though it was a 60-90 minute session, this replay of the memory felt like hours. Eventually, we started working on it. When we did, it took a matter of minutes to turn it from a video clip into a photograph (a technique called rewind if you want to read Trevor's book all about it "Cognitive Hypnotherapy: What's that about and how can I use it?"). All the emotion was gone.

Now here's the consequences. The rest of the film doesn't make sense without that clip. That is why it is such a significant stick to remove in the Kerplunk game. All the marbles fell through.

So instead of feeling all buzzed up and happy I feel flat and miserable. The way I have always defined myself is based on this "burden" I carried which I no longer do. So my whole life I have been in what Trevor calls "a state of protection" and now I have nothing that needs protecting.

Dawn C. Walton

So now what do I do?

The answer is to fill the space with positives. Love, happiness, fun etc. But I don't know how. I have to learn. I have been trying over the last 6 weeks and made some great progress but not enough to deal with this huge void right now. My brain is used to misery. I am used to it rewarding misery. It is such a battle to stop it finding a way to fill that space with misery.

I will try. In fact, I will make this work. But it's really tough.

And that's where I'm at right now. As usual, I'll keep you posted on progress – in case you're interested.

Dawn C. Walton

1st August, 2011

Stimulation

So what I have learnt is that the absence of a negative does not make a positive.

My two sessions with the Cognitive Hypnotherapist (Note that this is hypnotherapy and different from CBT) have, to all intents and purposes, wiped out the negative, emotional impact of pretty much all of the memories that have been plaguing me for the last 20+ years.

For the first time in my life, every action is not taken 'despite' my past. I am free from it. My choices and actions are mine to take without the influence of anyone or anything else other than myself.

What freedom! What a release! I should be floating around like a cloud as I no longer have a care in the world.

But I'm not. In fact, I have been quite the opposite. I have been miserable, on edge, short-fused. In fact, I knocked a coffee over in my office this morning, and when the little one didn't leave the room after a couple of times of asking I absolutely bellowed at her to get out.

She left the room in tears. I stayed in the room in tears. I now officially feel like the most horrible mother on the planet. Shortly after I went and cuddled her and told

Nothing Needs to be the Way it's Always Been

her I was sorry. But that doesn't work in my head. After all, men who beat their wives often say they're sorry afterwards too, don't they?

Anyway, my point is that I do not feel like I'm buzzing, free, etc like I should feel.

And the reason is that taking away the negatives does not do anything other than leave a big empty space. When for 20+ years all your thoughts have been about surviving, coping and, apparently, dwelling on misery, then all you want to do is fill that empty space with what you know. Misery.

Very frustrating!

Now normally I would be mailing backwards and forwards with Trevor and he would be gently nudging me in the right direction and keeping me on track. But Trevor is on holiday for a couple of weeks so I'm flying solo and not doing a very good job, it seems.

And then, Sandra (lady behind Thinking Slimmer, trained by and partner in crime to Trevor) stepped in and offered her help. Sandra has joined me on this journey from the start, even joining me on the first session I had (at my request). It is thanks to her that I am a) losing weight and b) seeing Trevor.

We had a chat. And what was clear is that I need to be constantly stimulated mentally. I need to be learning and challenging myself. If I'm not, my thoughts turn inwards too much and have a tendency to be destructive. Work doesn't do this for me because I am not in the right job right now. I have fun with the little one but I need to be really challenged.

So she suggested a couple of things I could do and one of them was a brilliant idea. All through this process, I have been fascinated by how it works. I've read Trevor's books and asked him lots of questions along the way, using my experience to understand the techniques he uses.

He has a bunch of training courses in the Quest Institute he runs, but also has some online stuff. One of the courses is WordWeaving, which is the magic behind what he does. It's an online course and affordable for me. So I signed up.

I started the first module this afternoon and already I feel better. I have something new to learn. Something I can get my teeth into and, hopefully, make some use of in the future.

So here's hoping I can build on this and fill the void with a new sense of who I am. Because right now, with all this freedom to choose I have no clue where to even start.

2nd August, 2011

Team building

Today I had a meeting with my team. I like meetings that I run. I can make them fun as well as informative.

The meeting went well despite the fact it was bucketing down (and yes, I know the rest of the UK was complaining it was too hot!).

Another positive was for the first time ever, I felt reasonably comfortable packed into a room with 12 other people. I didn't need to keep guarding myself against accidental physical contact. By jove, I think I might be getting somewhere!

So we did a team building exercise that involved competing to build the tallest structure out of wine gums, spaghetti and marshmallows (and scoffing the sweets after!).

And yesterday the hubby went to Tesco's with the little one and bought me this top. It's fitted. I NEVER wear fitted clothes because they show off all the bulgy bits! But I asked on Twitter and Facebook for an honest opinion and everyone said it looked smart. So I was brave.

And that was my day today. I even went for a run when I got home but I only managed to run the first mile and walk most of the second because the rain had made the path all soft. It was like running on sand!

Dawn C. Walton

7th August, 2011

Going nowhere

It's now been over a week since my second session with Trevor and I've been putting off writing this post.

I want to keep track of progress on this blog and in the 6 weeks between the first session and the second progress was amazing. There were lows but there were definitely more highs.

With this in mind, I went into the session over a week ago with high expectations of how my life would be looking by now.

Unfortunately, these expectations have not been met.

And I don't actually understand why.

As with Session 1, Session 2 was amazing. Afterwards it was clear that we had cleared off one more significant issue that I had been carrying around and I almost immediately felt very different about myself and my relationship with those around me. I no longer fear physical contact and can be around groups of people without constantly guarding against them getting too close to me.

I can stand and look in the mirror without hating what I see.

Nothing Needs to be the Way it's Always Been

I should be feeling great, shouldn't I? I should be buzzing. I should be looking forward to what I can do with my life without all these constraints that have held me back.

And yet…

…it's the opposite.

I feel like my life is pointless.

I am no longer spending my life looking back, getting through each day.

But I see nothing when I look forward. Each day looks the same and quite frankly it's mundane. I achieve nothing with work other than bringing in the money to support my family. I plod through each day without achieving anything.

I guess I always felt I had "something" that kept me going. Since the work I've done with Trevor, I am no longer constantly battling my past. It's not an issue any more. This is amazing. But it has left me empty. I have nothing to battle with! Isn't it ridiculous that I am complaining about this? Why can't I just appreciate what I have? Why can't I be happy?

After all I have everything I could possibly want. A wonderful husband whom I love dearly. The most amazing little girl. As much security in work as you get these days. A nice home. Some great friends.

I'm so pathetic that I can't appreciate all this and am still wallowing in the misery.

I hope the next blog post about this is way better than this one.

Dawn C. Walton

9th August, 2011

The power of the mind

Our brains are amazing.

I have known this for a long time but as time goes on I increasingly recognise just how amazing our minds are.

Yesterday I tweeted a photo. I saw a plane flying from right to left. Then Nik came back and he saw an eagle-type flying from left to right and Lex saw a jay type of bird.

Each of us interprets the same set of inputs in a different way. We each see the world differently and this is fundamental to the approach Trevor uses in Cognitive Hypnotherapy. Three people may experience the same thing, but because each person is unique, their interpretation of those experiences will be different.

This means that in therapy, you won't be very successful if you assume that you know the "fix" for everyone's problem because you've seen it before.

Each of us is different.

Our minds can create pain or eliminate pain.

Our minds can see things that don't exist or not see things that do.

Nothing Needs to be the Way it's Always Been

What is clear, and what Trevor is always telling me, is that our minds are malleable. We have the opportunity to change anything.

Did you realise that for the first 13 years or so of our lives we remember things pretty much in a binary way? It did or it didn't happen. The rest of our lives are then spent overlaying our adult interpretation over these memories to give them shades and significance and meaning. Every time something happens that causes us to reference one of these memories (good or bad) we add a little more colour to it and make it a little more 3-dimensional before we store it away again for future use.

So…I started on a journey over 7 weeks ago. I let Trevor have the fun of playing with the "silly putty" that is my brain. And he's pretty good at it. So changes were instant. I liked the new shape and the way I looked at the world because of it. I learnt to work with the different shape and appreciate some of the changes.

Then a couple of things happened and my "silly putty" got bent out of shape again. It wasn't what I was familiar with and it wasn't what Trevor moulded.

So I went to session 2 and once more we prodded and moulded.

This time, it was unrecognisable. There was nothing left of the familiar shape.

Quite honestly? I didn't like it. It was too unfamiliar. I had no tags or comparisons for how the shape now looked. I had no words to describe it.

"It's like, erm well…I don't know".

Dawn C. Walton

So then I wondered. Who am I? What matters to me? And I felt lost.

And this made me miserable.

We get comfort from those things that are familiar. Whether they are physical or mental. This is why my mind is so keen to hang on to misery. It's what I've always known.

And I see now.

I see the plane and the eagle and the jay.I see the sailing boat and I see a cloud.

I see that I have something new to work with here and that it's my choice what I do with that next.

I don't know what that choice will be. I need to think about that. But it's not a reason to be miserable. It's a reason to be excited. I have a sky full of clouds and each cloud is a possibility.

Watch this space because I think things are just about to get interesting.

12th August, 2011

A different flavour of misery

Last night, for the first time in over 3 years, the hubby and I went out to dinner together while my friend babysat (thank you, thank you, thank you).

We went to a little restaurant over in St Andrews that does Tex Mex kind of food including lovely steaks.

It was brilliant to get out. I had the chicken kebab skewer which looked amazing. However, it was undercooked. Not good. Sent it back and got nachos with chilli instead but by then I was stuffed and the hubby had well finished his meal. He had the steak which he thoroughly enjoyed and, to be honest, that's all that really matters. It's not like I eat much these days anyway!

It was lovely to get out and sit and talk. I love chatting to my hubby. It's what our relationship is based on but we don't get much of a chance these days.

I was, of course, talking about how amazing the last couple of months have been after the stuff with Trevor. How I couldn't believe what a difference it had made.

"Yeah, you do evangelise about it a lot", he said. *ahem* sorry about that. And then

"It's hard for me to see it working because you are still just as miserable."

I thought for a moment and realised he's right. I feel massively different. You see for me, it's a different flavour of miserable but how would anyone else know that? Let me try and explain how it works now. It's in 2 parts.

1. **Habit:** For over 20 years my head has been filled with miserable thoughts. Each day has been about surviving and making sure no one knew what was going on in my head. I never looked forward. It was an achievement to survive. Now, all those things that drove the misery are gone. I have absolutely no emotional driver of my misery. I am free of self-hatred, emotional pain etc. BUT you don't just stop something that has been a habit for so long. It's what my brain knows. It's what my brain is comfortable with. I am very aware I don't need to be miserable but I have to re-train my brain and teach it how to be happy. I have definitely had moments of genuine happiness. I just need to build on those until my brain is re-trained.

2. **Coping:** Up until now, nothing could touch me. The 'noise' created by my misery drove all other emotions and feelings into the dark, deep recesses of my brain. Now that noise is silenced, those feelings have a voice again. A voice I am not used to listening to and coping with. This means I am experiencing things in a way I never have before. And I'm learning how to cope in a whole new way. I'm learning to listen to the feelings and work with them instead of burying them.

Dawn C. Walton

This means that smaller things have a bigger impact than they have ever had before. So, for example, things that stress me. I've never really done stress before. There was very little that could compare to the way I was constantly feeling so stress was a small squeak. Now I get stressed. Little things stress me out. And it takes me longer to work out how to cope, to pick myself up and move on.

So you see, it may seem like I'm miserable but it's a totally different flavour. It's actually a positive thing! And it will get less and less. I will learn to be more and more positive. In fact, I predict in the future you'll be a bit sick of my positive posts and tweets!

And now it gets even better.

I have just signed up to do the Quest Institute Diploma in Cognitive Hypnotherapy. It's 1 weekend a month for 10 months and held in London, so quite a commitment.

But aside from the personal improvements, I have been fascinated by the approach since I first started talking to Trevor on email. And I love learning. I recently completed the WordWeaving online course (although still nervously waiting to see if I passed!) and really loved it.

So whether I use it just for learning and personal development or whether I do something with it, it will be brilliant. And I can carry on doing my job while I train, which is perfect.

Dawn C. Walton

14th August, 2011

Screen burn-in

Ever since the invention of the personal computer and the GUI (graphical user interface) we have had screen savers. It was soon clear that if you left an image on the computer screen for too long, those little glowing pixels eventually permanently burnt an image into the surface of the screen.

There are many similarities between our brain and computers and I think this is another one.

I have already spoken here about how, in my last session with Trevor, we released another mass of marbles in my backwards game of Kerplunk. I have been struggling with the empty space that remains.

And it occurred to me that it is very much like the burn-in you (used to?) get on a PC monitor. The original image is no longer being projected or displayed but you can still see it. It's no longer 3 dimensional. It's a bit blurry round the edges and certainly not strong enough for you to do anything with it – but every time you look it's there. And it's kind of annoying. Because it shouldn't be there.

After my first session I was buzzing. There was still a lot to work through but I was finding moments and was able

Nothing Needs to be the Way it's Always Been

to totally move on from those memories that had been holding me back for so long. I no longer needed answers because the questions weren't relevant. I found peace, at least from a good chunk of stuff. I know my hubby couldn't see it, but there was a huge change in me.

The second session was very different. We did something different, and worked on something different. This memory was deeply emotional and the real benefit of removing the emotion was not so much in terms of how I feel about myself but more about how I feel around others - the level of comfort I have with physical contact. It worked. Brilliantly. My first meeting with a group of people showed me I didn't have that fear any more that someone would grab my arm or sit too close. Again, not a very visible change to others but massive for me.

But now I am left with a type of screen burn-in. There is nothing left. Nothing there. But still I am left with an image. Still I am left with residual feelings.

I'm working on it. It's a little bit 2 steps forward, then 1 step back.

And today I made another couple of steps forward. For me, it's about understanding what is happening and why. But today I managed to have fun and relax and enjoy my day with the little one. Each time I do this, it helps me move forward. It's like kicking in the screen saver to start wiping out the burn-in.

I can see how far I've come. I really am a different person. I just need to somehow let that out more so that those around me can see it to.

Dawn C. Walton

18ᵗʰ August, 2011

A new Dawn - A bit of a summary

I've been thinking how I write this post. How do I summarise what I have learnt about myself in the last couple of months?

I have booked what I expect to be my last session with Trevor in the middle of October. That will be session number 3 and all is sorted.

My life has been lived, like the lives of all of us, based on a set of beliefs I formed as a result of childhood experiences. For many people, these beliefs are positive, reinforcing ones. Beliefs that give them the confidence to interact with the world and be who they want to be.

This was not the case for me.

My beliefs were

1. That I was impossible to love.

2. That I was impossible to even like.

I used my experiences as "evidence m'lord" in support of these two beliefs. I then took out of every interaction, whether with strangers or friends, further evidence to reinforce these core beliefs.

Nothing Needs to be the Way it's Always Been

By the time I was 18, I learned that emotions were just too risky and painful, and developed a technique for shutting them down totally. This stopped me experiencing the bad stuff, but also meant that I wasn't open to any of the good stuff that emotions can bring. I was an emotional black hole. This made it hard to get close to me. Something I was both reassured by, and also further evidence to support the case of belief number 2.

And so it perpetuated. All evidence against my beliefs was quickly explained away. The unconditional love that I have always had from my hubby has always been the hardest to reconcile – but in the absence of logic I managed to just not think about it. It could not be real.

I learnt to project an image of who I would like to be. An image that everyone would see and that would protect me from getting hurt. After all, if anything happened to an image, if someone didn't like an image, it really didn't matter.

And so I functioned. Inside, each moment that passed was less of an achievement and more of a disappointment. I took pride in my ability to hide how I felt, to do well at work, to ride any storm. Despite…

But that is not living. That is surviving. And somewhere, deep inside of me, there was the real me. Looking for opportunities to escape the prison I had built myself.

I saw a therapist for a year. I lost weight. I don't know why I did those things if I didn't value myself. But I did.

And then, one day, having read a number of blog posts about Thinking Slimmer, I decided to give it a bash. It seemed like I didn't have to do very much.

Dawn C. Walton

After a few days, I decided it wasn't going to work for me. Because of some of my childhood experiences. Because when I am depressed I starve myself – I don't eat. Because my relationship with food is emotional like many of us, but is also different.

I tweeted, that I wasn't sure it would work for me, as there were a few people discussing it. Sandra, who runs Thinking Slimmer called me and asked why I didn't think it would work for me. I gave her a vague answer, and a few hints which she picked up on. She explained that I needed to give it more time and told me about Trevor.

I thought on it for a day or two.

Then I told Sandra that I wanted to see Trevor.

Why did I do this? I'm not sure. I don't know what drives me to keep trying to fix myself. But the ball was rolling and once I start something I keep going, no matter how scary it is. I never turn away from any challenge.

For 2 weeks before my first appointment I mailed backwards and forwards with Trevor. Really trying to understand if he really could help me (I didn't believe he could at first). Sandra told me it usually took 2 or 3 sessions. I saw my therapist for over a year and it barely scratched the surface.

He patiently explained what he did, responded to an unending stream of questions from my side on how it worked and how it would work for me, so by the time we first met, we'd already got the size of each other pretty well!

Nothing Needs to be the Way it's Always Been

So we hit the ground running. And I was terrified.

You can read from my posts how the process has gone, but what about my two beliefs?

1. I do not believe I am un-lovable. I believe I was a child who was unlucky enough to end up with a pretty crappy family. For me, the evidence of bad experiences with a father/stepmother and then mother/stepfather combination had always been the ultimate evidence of why no one could love me. Now it is nothing but a story in a book that could be written about someone else. It proves nothing.

2. I am not un-likable. As a child, we adapt to our surroundings to survive. In the same way that a gazelle has to be able to walk quickly after being born to avoid predators, as a child I learnt to respond to the adults around me in the way that was best for my survival. I knew nothing else. Who I am was not defined by who they were and their flaws. It is up to me to choose that. I can be whoever I choose to be. Those people I interacted with in my adult life, that I chose to interpret as not liking me, either never had a chance, or actually did like me and I was just unwilling to accept it. I can see now that I know many amazing people who I have stayed in touch with across the miles and over the years and who have chosen to be my friends and remain my friends despite many opportunities to lose touch. Thank you to you all because you are truly amazing people and I can see now how lucky I am to have you in my life.

Dawn C. Walton

There is a lot of work still to do. I have not cracked this yet.

But for now, I am in a place where I know I will continue to move forward and learn to value myself and those around me. I will be able to experience a whole range of emotions and share them with the people around me that I love and care about so much. And in those emotions, there will be happiness and fun in abundance because that is just the coolest thing to feel, I've discovered.

Dawn C. Walton

24th August, 2011

Thinking Positive

I haven't really been posting many "Positive of the day" posts this week.

There is a very good reason for this – I haven't been positive.

I've been really struggling, in fact. It started with the hubby getting hurt by the little one again on Friday. And then on Monday it happened again. This time she climbed up in the chair behind him where he couldn't reach her and really hurt his back. I had to get her off and tell her off.

This has affected me in two ways.

Firstly, I have been really worried about the hubby. As mentioned in a previous post, I stress a lot over his well-being, especially when I have to travel. Whilst the little one understands not to touch his chest and back, and follows the rule 99% of the time, 1% of the time she's just a kid and ignores it. It's a game to her and the more he shouts, the more she giggles. And no, reward charts, naughty step, rational explanation, shouting all don't work. They work for a short while and then she adapts and gets bored. So I really worry and feel responsible for him.

Nothing Needs to be the Way it's Always Been

Secondly, in disciplining her, she cried. I feel like I've been very impatient with her lately too. This made me feel like a monster. I saw myself as my stepmother. I saw my stepmother hitting me and losing it with me constantly, I saw how I tiptoed around her and kept as quiet as possible because I could never do anything right. And I felt I was becoming her. I felt I was creating an environment of terror. When the little one was giggling and cuddling me later, when she called me wonderful and a superhero the next day, I felt like she was placating me. I had become evil.

I have been going round in this loop in my head. I just wanted to run away. To take myself away from the environment where I could spoil it for her.

…and yet…I'm still here.

Today I smiled again. Today I felt positive. Today, I do not feel like a monster.

Why? Did Trevor set me straight with one of his magic emails? Not this time.

Yes, I mailed him. But he's really busy and knows that he does not need to respond to me as quickly any more.

This time, I think, it was my unconscious that stepped in. All the reprogramming we have done. The listening to the latest track he has recorded for me every night. This time, my unconscious helped me out of it instead of throwing me in deeper.

I still am not sure if I am a monster or not. Certainly the little one shows no signs that I am. I will be more patient and I will eliminate some of those behaviours that I have hated seeing in myself. I will not be outsmarted by a 3 year old (albeit a smart, cute and funny one!). I can find a way to make her understand that doesn't involve shouting. That doesn't involve me hating myself after.

So this is my positive of the day. Today I found my way back to the happy place. On my own. And I am happy once again. Each time I do this, it becomes a little easier the next time.

Dawn C. Walton

27th August, 2011

The big switch

Last night as I went to sleep, for the first time in a couple of months, I didn't listen to any of the tracks Trevor has recorded for me in and around our sessions.

You see, I feel I am ready to let my own unconscious brain take over now. I think it has received the messages in the tracks and can learn on its own now.

This morning I woke up and felt, well, I think the best phrase is "a bit meh!".

Which is the way I have felt when I've woken up for weeks. Which is why I started running. Which is why I wrote about choosing your mood.

I have been increasingly frustrated by not feeling happy. By carrying a cloud of misery everywhere I go. Why? There is nothing wrong. I am, to all intents and purposes fixed.

And then I realised.

I can choose to be a happy person who occasionally feels miserable instead of a miserable person who occasionally feels happy.

Nothing Needs to be the Way it's Always Been

It's that simple. I just need to think of myself differently. This is, after all, about reprogramming my brain and that is down to me.

So that's it. As of today I am a happy person.

And do you know what? I think today has been a little easier because of that. Because up until now I have constantly been trying to understand what is wrong with me and why I am so miserable without reason. Today I didn't need to waste energy doing that because I'm not actually miserable! Hoorah!

Well, sort of. I may not be miserable but I'm not really happy either, but I'll work on that. I'm still learning!

Dawn C. Walton

31st August, 2011

Experts and learning

The Decisive Moment is the first book from my pile that I have been reading and I wanted to share a couple of key lessons that are actually quite applicable to me right now and have been reinforced by some recent communications with Trevor.

I am only halfway through the book so there is likely more to come but here's a little of what I have learnt.

Firstly the book examines the science and consequential behaviours around the human decision making processes. Are we driven by emotion or logic? What allows us to override instincts in certain situations? What makes a good decision-maker?

Lesson 1: It is fundamental to human nature to learn

One of the first things I found fascinating in this book is what the scientists call the "Oh shit" circuit (technical term anterior cingulate cortex ACC). A part of the brain that deals with things that we don't expect and as a result freaks us out. It is alerted by our Dopamine neurons that something didn't happen as expected (for example, feeling our car bang something when reversing when we thought the way was clear). It is alerted by a mismatch in what we know and what we feel (our brains are

Nothing Needs to be the Way it's Always Been

fundamentally a combination of emotional unconscious thought, and rational conscious thought) and it jumps into frantic action, kicking off all our systems in a panic, increasing the heart rate, making our palms sweaty etc. Isn't it amazing that there is a part of our brain that does this? It seems to me a bit like a survival circuit because it also helps us learn from these "oh shit" moments to make sure they don't happen again (I take more time to look when reversing next time). In days where all we had to worry about were hunting, eating and sleeping, I am sure this part of the brain would allow us to learn things like "don't try and hunt when your prey is downwind from you because they can smell you" etc. The is the first example of how critical learning is to us all.

Lesson 2: We should praise our kids for the effort they make and not their innate intelligence

The next lesson I learned has already changed both my behaviour and the hubby's around the little one. In this book, Lehrer refers to an experiment done by a Stanford psychologist called Carol Dweck to determine the impact of praise on kids. One by one, kids were taken out of a class and given a simple test consisting of non-verbal puzzles. After, half the kids were praised for their intelligence and the other half for their effort. They were then offered a choice of two subsequent tests. The first choice they were told was harder, but they'd learn a lot from attempting it. The other test was a simple one similar to the one they'd just taken. 90% of the kids praised for their effort chose to take the harder test while most of the kids praised for intelligence went for the simpler test. Interesting, isn't it? Her studies continued and eventually she showed that the kids praised for their efforts improved their fundamental test scores by an average of 30% while the ones praised for their intelligence didn't improve. We used to say "aren't you clever?" to the little one all the time. We have changed our language and now use phrases like "you did really well at that" or "well done for keeping at it".

Lesson 3: We should focus on what we learn from our mistakes and not the result we achieved at the end

We're all familiar with the concept of learning from our mistakes and we know that it's pretty much impossible to learn from other people's mistakes as effectively. We also may have a tendency to regard experts as those people who are all-knowing. Whereas, in reality, experts are usually people that have made lots of mistakes and learned from them – furthering their knowledge and expertise. For them, they will never be satisfied that they know everything, they will constantly be making mistakes and using them as an opportunity to learn. I think the most famous quote around this is the Thomas Edison quote *"I have not failed. I've just found 10,000 ways that won't work"*. In this book, Lehrer profiles a couple of people who are renowned for being the best in their field (TV and film directing and poker playing) and looks at what makes them so good at what they do. What is the decision process that allows them to make the right decisions? His conclusion seems to be that these are people who focus, not on what they have achieved, but on what they need to do better next time. I am in the middle of this right now. I have been struggling a lot this past week with a flood of memories that are niggling

Nothing Needs to be the Way it's Always Been

at me and making me feel sad. I have been turning it into "I'm being crap and useless". Even though, for the most part, the pain has been removed from these memories. And I've been getting really frustrated with myself for failing to move on. But, as Trevor keeps telling me, it's all about learning. I have managed to move on from using these as an opportunity to put myself down. I am now focussed on what they are all about and what I can learn from them. They might just still be the screen burn-in that I mentioned in a previous post, or maybe there really is something I can gain from them. A lesson to help me move on. I've not found it yet. But now I'm focussed on the learning I can gain, I have been able to step away from myself a little bit instead of being in the thick of it.

I really recommend this book if you are at all interested in how and why we think the way we do. It's an interesting and easy read with lots of practical case studies to make things clearer. I'm sure I'll be using it for more lessons and sharing more of it with you as I continue to read it.

Dawn C. Walton

1ˢᵗ September, 2011

I want...

I want to be held like I've never been held before

I want to be told I don't have to worry any more

I want to be loved in a way I've never let anyone do

I want to show my husband that I love him truly too

I want to believe that everything was meant to be

I want to believe in a reason for all that happened to me

I want to be happy, have fun, laugh out loud

I want to look at the person I've become and feel proud

I want to look forward to my future instead of back

I want to get through a day without giving myself flak

I want to take each day as a chance to learn and grow

I want to make a difference to the lives of those I know

I want to be a great person and mother and wife

I want to be more than an actor in the story of my life

I want to forgive myself for not being as good as I can be

I want to be able to appreciate and like just being me.

Nothing Needs to be the Way it's Always Been

I never wanted any of these things before because I was just surviving. Now I know what I want and I am on my way there…but I'm not there…yet…

Yesterday I was reading my book 'The Decisive Moment' and had been reading about the role of the prefrontal cortex in our thinking. It appears that this part of the brain is what distinguishes humans from animals because it deals very much with rational and logical thought processes. What was interesting is how psychologists have discovered that this part of the brain consumes a lot of energy, so when we are exhausted, we default back to our emotional and intuitive brain.

Suddenly a lot made sense. I struggle when I am tired to get out of a pattern of miserable thoughts. I get frustrated at myself because I am unable to rationalise over them. This last week, with the little one wanting to move away from night-time nappies and failing, my sleep has been constantly interrupted.

So I have been tired all day, meaning my prefrontal cortex does not have the energy it needs for effective rational thought (certainly not when I am working at the same time and using all my energy for that). So I am giving myself a "get out of jail free card" while I'm tired. I am lowering my expectations of myself and will work hard to not attribute any deeper meaning to miserable thoughts.

Dawn C. Walton

3ʳᵈ September, 2011

Forgive me, I'm perfect

I am perfect.

Aren't you? Go on, say it, "I am perfect".

What, you're not? Actually I'm not either. Not by a long shot.

So isn't it weird that I give myself such a hard time for my failings and failures?

Surely, if I can accept that I am not perfect (let's face it, not a difficult thing to accept) then as a consequence I must also accept that I will do things I am not happy with and will feel I can often do better?

Trevor has told me to "forgive myself" from the very first track he recorded for me. I have always laughed at the very thought (in that snorting ugly laugh kind of way). I have very high expectations of myself that I rarely meet!

And then, the other day, I read a part of 'The Decisive Moment' that gave me a serious light bulb moment.

You see this, week has been really tough because there hasn't been a single night where the little one slept through. I have been mega tired. The one night I got a solid sleep it was short and sandwiched in two 5 hour drives!

Nothing Needs to be the Way it's Always Been

I get very low when I am tired. And, up until recently, I have beaten myself up for not being in better control of my feelings.

Then I realised it was not my fault.

I forgave myself for feeling miserable. I lowered my expectations of myself…

…and do you know what happened? I have felt GREAT! Happy and light!

Because it's not my fault. Because I am not perfect.

So my Positive of the Day today is: Trevor was right – FORGIVE YOURSELF!

Go on try it…it's really hard to do but if you manage it you'll feel brilliant.

Dawn C. Walton

9th September, 2011

My name is Dawn and I am...

...HAPPY!

Something fundamental has changed in my head, and in fact in my life.

I never really dreamed when I started on this journey that it would actually work. I could never imagine what sort of person I would be if I didn't carry the burden of my past experience with me. That would require looking forward, and I have always lived with my eyes firmly planted on the ground. I was surviving each moment and dreading the next.

It has not been an easy journey but it has been amazing.

I need to understand why things work. From the very first moment I made contact with Trevor I have been constantly questioning him about how things will work and why things will work. He has patiently answered. Apparently he enjoys discussing and teaching this stuff – which has, I believe, been a key factor in how successful the therapy has been.

I am still trying to understand a couple of things. I am reading books and emailing Trevor but there are some things that still seem nothing short of magic. Maybe after my course I will understand them better.

Nothing Needs to be the Way it's Always Been

The biggest struggle for me has been to cope with a huge loss. The loss of the emotional attachment to my memories. You'd think I'd be grateful, wouldn't you?

I've lived for 20 years with a rot eating away at me. Every waking minute was filled with thoughts of self-loathing. All I wanted to do was escape from being me. I couldn't appreciate any of the wonderful things in my life because all I wanted to do was escape. There was a constant inner voice streaming out a diatribe of criticisms and insults that I was used to as a background noise. That I ignored as I got on with my life but that filled my head so there was little room for anything else in there. I didn't know what it felt like to be happy. I had never been happy. I didn't know it was possible to be any other way.

Then I had the first session with Trevor. As I sat in the airport after, waiting for my flight home, I was aware of a silence. The voice in my head had gone! Just like that. And I had never known the silence before. It was weird. I thought and pondered. As well as the voice vanishing, I no longer needed answers to the question "What is it about me that made it impossible for a mother, father, stepmother, stepfather to love me?". Because, for the first time in my life it didn't seem to matter. For the first time, I could see that maybe it wasn't actually about me and maybe it was more about them.

As the weeks went by, I struggled to cope with the emptiness in my head. Think about it, there was always noise and now there was silence. There were always questions and now there were none. Everything that I knew about myself had changed in the space of 90

Dawn C. Walton

minutes. As I listened to the track Trevor had recorded for me, every night, I found myself in turmoil. I was shaken, I was crying, I had a temper and a short fuse. The noise being gone had allowed the other things, the ones that had hidden quietly in a corner for years, to surface. I was responding emotionally to the world around me in a way I had never done before and it was scary.

I spent the weeks beating myself up for not feeling great. I should feel wonderful. The memories of my childhood were now a storybook. I shouldn't be miserable any more. And I struggled with the unfamiliar emotions.

And there were moments…brilliant moments where I connected with friends…where I felt lighter…where I could only whisper, for fear of consequences I couldn't define, "I'm happy right now".

And then, one evening, as I stood waiting for a kebab (I may eat less but I still eat crap!), a drunken guy came up behind me and put his arm round me. He muttered some unintelligible words and then left. I just about do hugs with the hubby, rarely with friends, random strangers are a no-no and unexpected drunken guys are cause for a meltdown!

The moments were gone. There was no more happiness until after my next session with Trevor. "It's good if you bring the fear with you to the session", Trevor said. "No problems", I replied, as I went into session 2 as a total wreck, feeling like all the good work had vanished out of the window.

After that session I went home and hugged the hubby. I told him I loved him and for the first time in my life it

Nothing Needs to be the Way it's Always Been

was comfortable for me. I went to a meeting a few days later and wasn't feeling jumpy around the people in the room who would reach out and touch my arm. For the first time in my life I was comfortable in my own skin. I could look in the mirror and not instantly look away in disgust.

…and yet. And yet I was still miserable. Clearly I loved the misery. I was filled by emptiness and silence and hadn't learned what to do with it. All I knew, all that was familiar was negative and destructive. I had no idea what to fill the empty space with and I was hugely frustrated at myself.

Then I read a book, and had a light bulb moment. I realised that I'm not perfect (ironic eh?) and lowered my expectations of myself. And suddenly something happened…

…I was no longer miserable. I was no longer giving myself a hard time for not feeling brilliant.

I was suddenly happy. And I still am! Since that moment, when I realised that I am who I am. There is nothing to analyse. The only expectations of me are the ones I put on myself and I had been setting the bar way too high.

Now if Trevor reads this, he will be smiling and saying "I told you so" because these are all things he has been telling me would happen from the start. And of course, despite trusting him and despite knowing how brilliant he is, I never believed him!

On the 23rd I have what I expect to be my last session with Trevor. That will make it 3 times I've visited him. In that time he's changed my life.

My name is Dawn and I am HAPPY. Thank you, Trevor.

Dawn C. Walton

22ⁿᵈ September, 2011

Easy as 1, 2, 3

Number 1 Harley Street

2 amazing people

3 cognitive hypnotherapy sessions

That's what it has taken to change my life.

After 38 years (39 in a couple of weeks!) my life has been turned around and is amazing!

Tomorrow I have my final Cognitive Hypnotherapy session with Trevor in London. Session number three. I was terrified before session number one and just as terrified before session number two. This one I am looking forward to. A sure sign that I'm at the end.

But I'm only at the beginning really because at the end of October I start my Diploma in Cognitive Hypnotherapy which will open up a whole new chapter in my life.

At the same time I am still going with Thinking Slimmer thanks to the amazing support from Sandra. I have now lost at least 3st 2lbs since I started on it 18 weeks ago.

I am looking at buying size 14 jeans because most of the size 16s are too big. I am still working my way through

Nothing Needs to be the Way it's Always Been

clothes in my wardrobe because I have been on a diet most of my life, it seems. But this isn't a diet. This is a new way of life and a new way of thinking.

And for the first time in a long time I am feeling very comfortable with who I am, both inside and out.

And I am happy.

It seems it's as easy as 1, 2, 3.

4 - Session 3

Dawn C. Walt

23rd September, 2011

I don't know how to write this

I have blogged since the very first day I embarked, with significant trepidation, on my journey to receive help from Trevor Silvester and his approach called Cognitive Hypnotherapy.

I have brought you with me on this journey.

It is good for me to read back and see how far I've come in such a short space of time. My first session was June. My second August. My 3rd today.

Finished.

And now I am lost for words.

All I can do is smile. Yep. Smile.

I am so ridiculously happy. And comfortable in myself.

As I sat today talking to Trevor in our final session, we discussed all sorts of things. But most of all we laughed and smiled. I laughed and smiled.

We had a couple of final small details to try and smooth out. But we talked about the books I am reading that he recommended. We talked about the course that I start on at the end of October. We talked about gadgets.

And when I left we had a quick hug.

ng Needs to be the Way it's Always Been

ˡ all of this was totally brilliant.

So I am lost for words because somehow, at this moment, words are way too inadequate to describe how I feel.

I can't possibly describe to you what a fundamentally different person I am now to just a few short months ago.

I can't possibly describe to you how excited I am about my future.

I can't possibly describe to you how lucky I feel to have met, and had help from, Trevor.

I can't find words to describe how grateful I am to him for all that he has done for me.

I can't find words to describe how amazing each moment of my day is right now.

I can't find words to describe my excitement about continuing to learn things that will help my family and friends also share in this happiness and have better lives.

There are no words.

For 20 years I have been broken and I thought I would always be that way.

But today I have been fixed.

That is something to laugh and shout about, don't you think?

Dawn C. Walton

27th September, 2011

Running reflections

The sky was on fire this morning. It was gorgeous.

I set out for my run and it was mild and still. As I came off the road and on to the path, I could see the sky ablaze with the sunrise in front of me and, not for the first time, wished my eyes could take photos.

I smiled to myself as I looked forward to my run and began to reflect on how my life has changed so much lately.

I looked along the path, breathing easily (it was early in the run!) and enjoying the deep pink sky. The rest of the sky is grey and cloudy and if I hadn't gone for this run I would never have known about the gorgeous sunrise.

I randomly swallowed flies and swept spider webs out of my face. The spiders have been busy. Despite the music being played through my headphones I could hear the crows cawing and the thud of my feet on the muddy path.

I smiled again, thinking of the spider webs, as I felt like Indiana Jones running away from a temple being chased by a giant rock!

But for the first time, I'm not running away from anything.

Nothing Needs to be the Way it's Always Been

I am running towards something. I decided that today would be a 5km run because the conditions are so perfect and once more I look forward to the path ahead. I can do this. This is easy. 3 miles before I get going on my day. Oh how times have changed.

I smile again.

The path ahead reminds me to think of my future and the path I am now on.

In less than a month I attend the first weekend of my Diploma in Cognitive Hypnotherapy training. I am hugely excited. I love learning and I love that I can learn something that will help others. I have already benefited from what I have learnt so far. Both for me and those I care about.

I am all ready. I am getting a new iPad2 for my birthday in a couple of weeks for taking notes during the course and for doing Facetime with the little one and the hubby while I'm away. I have a Powermat coming for charging up all my technology. I have the right bag and new Doc Marten boots so I can walk to my friend's house from the station on a Saturday evening and Sunday morning. I am ready.

And I know now that this is my future.

I run comfortably past the 1 mile marker. It's not a fast pace at just under 12 minutes but it's good enough. I keep going.

I will become a Cognitive Hypnotherapist when I finish my training. I will initially practise at weekends and evenings. I will be doing something hugely worthwhile with my life. I will be doing for others what Trevor has done for me.

I reach the 1.6 mile point on the path and turn around and come back. I would prefer not to retrace my steps but there is no real option.

Besides, when you approach things from a different direction they look very different, don't they?

It's a different path in this direction. I take a different route to avoid the really muddy patches. The spider webs have now been broken. The sunrise is over and the sky is just grey. My breathing is heavier and I am sweating now. But I'm still running. This is easy. I can do this.

As I pass the 2 mile marker I remember how I used to have to stop and walk at this point but now I keep running. I reach 2.5 miles and have a hill to climb. A hill I used to walk up but now I run. I just keep going.

3 miles pass and I join the road again. I begin to sprint the last 100 yards or so to my house. My arms are pumping and I am breathing heavily and sweating.

I can do this. I feel good.

Oh how my life has changed. I am told the best is yet to come but for now, things are looking pretty good.

Dawn C. Walton

4th October, 2011

Feel first, think later

We like to think that our rational brain is in control of everything we do.

I'm sorry but I've got bad news for you: we're wrong.

Think of something you're scared of. Spiders, for example.

When you see a spider, do you stand there and think "hmm, it's only tiny. It doesn't bite. I can squish it with my shoe".

Or does your heart start racing as you feel the sudden urge to run away screaming like a girl (even if you aren't one) and leap on to the nearest chair, seeking high ground to get away from the person-munching beastie (incidentally, have you noticed they can climb walls and stuff?).

If you're lucky, you might eventually regain control and start overriding your emotions (usually when someone has removed the beastie) and return to your normal rational state. If the fear is really deep-rooted it will get worse and those rational thoughts won't get a look in.

You see, we generally feel first and think later.

Nothing **Needs to be the Way it's Always Been**

This shows us that our unconscious mind is our primary master.

This is why the introduction of flight simulators for training pilots has been so effective in reducing accidents. They can feel first, think later in an environment where there are no consequences. Then they can do it again and again until they are familiar enough with a whole range of scenarios that there is no initial emotional response.

So this "feel first" thing comes from our unconscious. And it builds a whole matrix throughout our childhood in response to events. It essentially is programmed to look after us, to do what it thinks is best to protect us. We then spend the rest of our lives rationalising over the feelings that come from our unconscious.

Because we feel first, think later, we usually don't really understand why we feel the way we do. Of course we don't. It's not like we can start an instant messaging conversation with our unconscious.

RB: *"Erm hello unconscious"*

U: *"Oh hey there Rational Brain, how's it going?"*

RB: *"Well not too good, actually. I have to present to loads of people today and I'm bricking it. Quite frankly, I'm confused because I really know my stuff and these are all people I chat with all the time. Could really use feeling calmer right now"*

U: *"Oh right…erm…"*

RB: *"I don't suppose you have any ideas of what I can do to calm myself down do you? I am trying to breathe and stuff"*

Dawn C. Walton

U: "Are you sure you want to do this? I mean, there was that time when you were singing at school and you forgot the words, wasn't there?"

RB: "Oh, I'd forgotten that"

U: "Yeah I was there. I remember it really well. You got really upset and ran off the stage crying"

RB: "Gosh yes, so I did. But I was only 5"

U: "Yeah but you wouldn't want that to happen again, would you? Best avoid those kinds of thing again, eh? I'm only trying to look out for you here"

RB: "But you see, Unconscious, I still have to present whether you like it or not. So don't you worry about me. Just let me get on and do it. I'm 35 now not 5 so I'll be fine now"

U: "Hmmm, I'm really not sure about this. I don't want you to get hurt again"

RB: "OMG U, did you not listen? I'm 35! I should be able to get up on the stage and present by now!"

U: "Geez, no need to get all stroppy with me. I'm just looking out for you. Fine. If you wanna be like that, I'll leave you to it. On your head be it if you forget your words again"

RB: "Thank you, that's all I wanted!"

That would be useful, wouldn't it?

This is why Cognitive Hypnotherapy is so useful. And in fact, this is why Thinking Slimmer works so well.

It works with the reality that our unconscious thoughts live in and helps us reframe and redefine the

Nothing Needs to be the Way it's Always Been

interpretations and conclusions that it reached when we were younger. This is why the Hypnotherapy part is key, because that's how we start the Instant Messaging session with the unconscious.

By reframing those significant events that our unconscious has used throughout our lives to drive the "feel first, think later" approach, we remove the emotional reactions to events or stimuli in our daily lives. Without the emotional reaction, there is no need to "think later" because we haven't even had the "feel first".

This is also why many of us struggle for years to overcome those things that make every day a struggle. The things that drive depression or make it hard for us to connect with others. Because we can only work on our conscious mind. We can rationalise and think our way through it all. We can decide we don't need to feel like this. But then all it takes is one key stimulus and our unconscious overrides all our good work. We feel first and think later.

Dawn C. Walton

18ᵗʰ October, 2011

Looking forward not backwards

As you know, I had my last session with Trevor about a month ago.

It was kind of a 'mop up' session but one of the things we discussed was the fact that whilst I no longer hate myself, I still am failing to see myself in the positive.

I can say "I am not…"

But I can't say "I am…"

So the recording Trevor did for me from session 3 focussed on helping my unconscious focus on the good things I have achieved.

For whatever reason, unlike all other tracks that I have had from Trevor, including the Thinking Slimmer ones, this one just didn't seem to take hold. Rather than my residual thoughts being positive (you know the ones, when your head is not occupied by something else, these are the ones that bounce around your head randomly!) it seems I have been finding even more reasons to feel pants about myself.

And it's a habit of a lifetime that is very hard to break. Despite feeling good and positive about life.

Nothing Needs to be the Way it's Always Been

Despite appreciating the moments. Despite looking ahead to my future and actually planning for the first time ever what I want to do next.

But here's the thing: I am at a point now where I should be able to manage this through myself. I have read around. I have experienced. I may not start my course until this weekend (oooohhhhh exciting!) but I know enough now to recognise what triggers these thoughts, why I think them and how I can move on from them. So I have done a list in an attempt to move forward.

It was interesting to write. Because it was a struggle to find the things under the "I am not…" category. Maybe I should add: "I am not good at seeing what is right in front of me!"

Dawn C. Walton

19th October, 2011

The battle of man vs food

There is a programme on one of the Sky food channels called Man vs Food.

I love this programme.

Basically, this guy, Adam, goes around America taking on challenges to eat the biggest plates of food. Things like burgers, hotdogs and even soups are laid before him in huge mountains. As he eats until he practically bursts, I drool over the delicious food that he is scoffing.

I love food. I love the taste of it. I love the freedom of being able to eat it.

When I was a young child, food was not readily available. Not because we were poor but because my parents couldn't be bothered. My brother and I were far from their top priority and so the only place we were guaranteed of getting a solid meal was at school. And boy, did we make the most of that. We would have second and third helpings every day but remained extremely thin until later when we went to live with my mother.

As a result, food has a really special place in my life.

Nothing Needs to be the Way it's Always Been

I remember all events from the early part of my life based on the food I had.

One day, before school, my father made us breakfast. He never usually did this. We had Weetabix and, as I remember, we somehow got two lots. We both kept very quiet about it but because it was so unusual, when I got to school I was really sick. They wanted to send me home but I refused to go. I was sick in the sink in our classroom so I did not need to go home to get changed. I still thought it was great that we got 2 lots of breakfast, though.

At Christmas we would sometimes get a segment or two of a satsuma. I used to suck all the flesh out of it and then chew on the remaining skin for hours like it was chewing gum. It always made it feel like I was getting a lot more food that way! My hubby always laughs at me and says I should write a book on "the correct way to eat stuff" because I have technique for eating everything.

Once, before we were due to be picked up by my mother and her husband for a school holiday custody visit, my stepmother came up to us playing outside and gave us each a Wagon Wheel. I had not had one before and found it really nice – but I think it was stale. It tasted stale – but hey, food was food so I scoffed it anyway.

One Easter my brother and I were sat together at the far end of the land around our house. Normally this area was out of bounds and certainly the area beyond it was, so I have no idea why we were there. It was evening and I recall that we were sent up there for some reason. We had been huddled there sheltering behind a mound

Dawn C. Walton

of grass to escape a nippy breeze, when my stepmother appeared. In her hand she had two of those mini-Easter eggs that are covered in foil with a face painted on it and Smarties inside. We were, to say the least, shocked (and delighted). I still have no idea what we were doing there but I definitely remember the Easter eggs!

When I was a little older we took a trip to the park with my parents and grandparents. I found a £5 note on the ground. This was unusual because it was my brother that was the lucky one. Anyway, I bought everyone an ice cream with the money…but the top fell off mine…

As I grew older and got some control over what I could eat, I naturally put on a load of weight. I could eat whatever I wanted to and that is exactly what I did. I loved food and still do.

When I was having a particularly hard time, I stopped eating. That was the only control I had. When I was suffering from stress, the physical symptoms showed themselves in my stomach and I was sick every morning when I tried to go to school (cue the morning sickness jokes from everyone, of course!).

By the time I went to Uni I had been ill for a couple of years and lost a lot of weight. At Uni I was fine. The sickness disappeared and I started playing squash, sometimes a few times a day. At that point I was around a size 10 and the healthiest I have ever been.

I learnt that I could eat what I wanted as long as I exercised enough to balance it out.

Nothing Needs to be the Way it's Always Been

Since then, all through my life, my weight has been a challenge due to not being able to keep up the level of exercise that cancels out my eating.

To diet, for me, is punishing myself. To deprive myself of food is like taking me back to my childhood where I had no choice. At the same time, I never learnt how to regulate my intake of food because I was always so limited on what was available. When I was young, I rarely had the opportunity to eat until I was full.

When I started Thinking Slimmer, I was sure it wouldn't work for me for all of these reasons.

But for me, it is the perfect solution. It has tapped into my unconscious and allowed me to understand those signals that tell me I'm full before I eat so much that I could explode. It has activated my unconscious so I don't need to snack and constantly prove that I can eat now.

I have now got a far more natural approach to food consumption and I don't have to deprive myself to achieve a balanced weight. I can still eat the food I like but I don't want to eat too much of it.

I don't believe there is any other solution out there that would have worked like this for me.

Thinking Slimmer has allowed me to be normal.

Dawn C. Walton

25th October, 2011

I'm a baby giraffe

I can appreciate that when you look at me, your first thought is not "gosh she looks like a baby giraffe".

Not really surprised by that.

But you see, these days I share many of the qualities of a baby giraffe.

What am I banging on about now?

Well, up until relatively recently, I avoided all elements of physical contact with the people around me like the plague. If someone reached out and touched my arm or hand, as is common in normal social interactions, it was like someone tasered me. It would set off a sequence of events in my head to cancel out my "oh help, let's get the hell out of here" response.

For a few moments, I would become totally internally focussed. All resources would be directed to not letting on what I was feeling, not running away and getting to a point where I could re-engage in the 'now'.

Notice that this is written in the past tense.

These days, it is not an issue. I barely notice if someone is in contact with me. Even on the tube etc, I am very relaxed about it. I do notice, but only to be amused by how different it is for me now.

And therein lies my problem.

This is where I become a bit like a baby giraffe.

When they are born they are all legs, ungainly and wobbly. It seems like it is just too much for them to learn how to coordinate that body of theirs?

Have I suddenly started having difficulty controlling my legs? Well no, not really. But I have that same level of awkwardness. I watch people and they walk into a room and give someone a hug or just stand by them and rest their hand on the person's arm or shoulder. And I marvel at it. Because they do it unconsciously. They connect and it is amazing. I have been watching in awe at how natural it is for everyone to just connect.

You see, I don't know how.

I have never done it.

It feels massively awkward and I worry about getting it all wrong and, to be honest, I am likely to physically run away and hide with embarrassment if I do get it wrong in some way.

And so essentially nothing has changed. To all intents and purposes I still have my "Back off, buddy" shield up and I am not choosing to 'engage' because I don't know how. I am worried about being way too much like a baby giraffe with legs all over and falling over all the time!

Dawn C. Walton

7th November, 2011

Hugs and Copying

The little one loves to hug.

I was reminded of this over the weekend when Susan and her lovely family visited and the little one gave Susan a lovely hello and goodbye hug. And when my friend visited, the little one ran and gave her a hug as soon as she came through the door. She is brilliant to hug. I get the most wonderful warm engulfing feeling when she's in my arms. Sometimes, it is so special, it even makes me cry with happiness.

The little one loves to copy.

She watches and studies people and TV shows. She processes and then she applies in her own unique way. We have to watch what she's watching so we can predict what she is going to do!

What's my point?

Well, if the little one loves to copy and the little one loves to hug, then I'm not doing such a bad job. As a non-hugger it is clear that my hang-ups have not rubbed off on the little one yet. And now things are changing, then maybe they never will.

It's just a thought.

Dawn C. Walton

13th November, 2011

Reality and Belief

One of the things that has always impressed me about Trevor is that he doesn't engage in what I say. You can see that he is always working out how he can make use of information, rather than trying to persuade me that I am wrong in what I am saying. Because there is no point arguing with someone's version of reality.

For example, when someone says to you "I'm a crap mother", if you're like me, then you're most likely to respond with "No, you're not" and then would go on with a list of examples that I have seen why you are a good mother.

However, this is a bit futile. Why? Because it is your belief and nothing that I say will change that belief. It is your view of reality. It is your life and how accurate or true it appears to me has nothing to do with it. Whatever you believe is the truth.

If you believe you are fat, then in *your* reality you are.

There are a number of techniques in Cognitive Hypnotherapy that allow us to work with the unconscious brain to redefine that reality and build a new, often less negative and damaging one. Sometimes this is about reprogramming the unconscious to

Nothing Needs to be the Way it's Always Been

interpret its thoughts differently. Sometimes it is about taking the emotion out of the memories or thoughts that effectively wipes them from your reality.

As I have been on my own journey, and then more so as I have started my course and read more, I have realised that I have a strong set of these negative beliefs that may actually only hold me back.

For example:

"I will not restrict the sort of things that I eat because to do so would make it impossible for me to lose weight. I need to eat whatever I want to have control"

"I will never be as good as anyone else at anything I do"

"I will not set myself goals because I will fail and I can't handle failure"

I could go on for a long time here. It doesn't matter what anyone says – this is my reality. Disagreement with it just gives me something to kick back against.

As I embark on this new journey, in my head, I am already classing myself as a failure. You can see from my write-up of the first weekend how I have already found all those opportunities where I have failed and others haven't. It is my natural response to learning anything new. I want so much to be good at what I do that I put myself at the bottom of the pile and allow myself to fail. In fact, I expect it.

This is quite a behaviour change I need to achieve. Next weekend is weekend 2 of my course. I have another

Dawn C. Walton

9 months to learn to become better at improving myself. At thinking positively.

Nothing has to stay the same as it's always been.

Anything can be changed.

And I will be changing my reality, it's just going to take some time, hard work and a lot of honesty with myself to do it!

17th November, 2011

World prematurity day

It seems that today is world prematurity day, raising awareness of premature babies.

I have been thinking about Adam a lot recently. More than usual although I'm not sure why.

Since Trevor helped me, I am comfortable with these thoughts and can handle processing them in my normal daily stream of thoughts. They hurt. But I can ride it through. It's not the same for the hubby and one day, I hope to help him too. Although I am not sure I can do it with the skill that Trevor did.

We call 2007 "two thousand and shit"

Here's what happened.

In **December**, my much-loved cat Ratty developed a tumour on his kidney which we didn't know about. All we knew was in the space of 2 weeks he went from a lovely big fluffy black and white cat to skin and bones with no bladder control. We took him to the vet and they said there was nothing they could do and we walked out of the vet without him. I was distraught. He was the first pet I had lost and he left such a hole in our lives.

Nothing Needs to be the Way it's Always Been

At the same time the hubby was really ill over Christmas. He could barely eat. We thought it was a really bad flu and he refused to see a doctor. We had a friend to stay and we went out for the day leaving the hubby at home. On the way I got a phone call from him. He couldn't breathe. I called an ambulance and raced back to find the ambulance crew walking my hubby down the steps to the van, and him clearly struggling terribly. The ambulance crew suggested it was just flu and we could wait and see the doctor or have him taken to hospital. I opted for the latter.

As it was over Xmas, no one cared. They did some tests, admitted him, treated him for flu and sent him home (we now know he'd had a heart attack). He didn't get better. He eventually saw a doctor after much persuasion who also said flu. He still didn't get better. He eventually, after much persuasion, went back to the doctor and got a decent one. This doctor knew what it was straight away and sent him for a treadmill test at the hospital. He had a heart attack while doing the test and they admitted him to Cardiac Intensive care in **January**. They did an angiogram and discovered 3 blockages in the arteries to his heart. They scheduled him for a heart bypass operation in **February** in Aberdeen.

At this point we discovered I was pregnant.

He went to Aberdeen hospital and I booked into a local Premier Inn. On the day of his op they cancelled because they didn't have any Intensive Care Unit beds and sent us home.

Dawn C. Walton

We heard nothing for a month. We chased. We heard nothing. We discovered that they thought he had already had the op and hadn't put him back on the list. They gave us a new date of July. There was every chance he wouldn't live that long.

We paid for him to go privately, which was the best decision we ever made. In **March** 2007 he had a quadruple heart bypass operation in a private hospital in Glasgow. I drove back and forth every day he was there.

While he was in for his operation I had my 12-week scan and all looked good.

He came out of hospital and had problems with his legs healing for nearly 3 months. They remove veins from the legs to rebuild the ones to the heart and his just weren't healing.

The 20-week scan in **June** was OK but he wouldn't move at all. In fact, I now know, after having the little one, that he wasn't moving as much as was usual anyway. But it was my first pregnancy so I didn't know.

At 24 wccks, now in June, I went for a check-up with the midwife and they had concerns about my blood pressure. I went into hospital. I told them it was the stress of being in hospital that wasn't helping. I hate hospitals and I hated all the physical contact around being pregnant. It was hugely stressful for me. Again, so was my hubby nearly dying, with hindsight!

I was then in and out of hospital for days at a time until the day I turned 26 weeks pregnant when they did a scan where it showed the blood flow to his head was not good

Nothing Needs to be the Way it's Always Been

enough. They told me the only option was to deliver. On **July** 6th, 2007, my world collapsed as I was booked in for an emergency C-section.

The delivery went fine. He even cried when they got him out. We thought this was a good sign but it meant nothing. He was 1lb 6oz.

The first night the hubby slept in my room as the doctors told us he was about to die. He didn't.

In fact, despite being told almost every day "he's going to die today" by the doctors, he lived for 30 days. At one point the hubby and I were discussing the practicalities of bringing him home. But everything was against us and when one of his medicine feeds leaked causing a caustic burn on his arm, it was just one more thing than he could fight against. All his energy that was focussed on surviving now had to deal with this and it was downhill from there. It wasn't anyone's fault. Their veins are so tiny and so many things were in his veins.

On **August** 5th, after being given a steroid injection to give his lungs a chance, he developed a tear in his stomach lining and was in a lot of pain. We always said we would do everything for him but if he was suffering we wouldn't let that happen. There was nothing that could be done.

At 1am he was dosed up with morphine and we turned off his ventilator.

We both hoped against hope that he would breathe – but of course he never was going to.

Dawn C. Walton

This was my only cuddle with him and my only regret in life will remain that I didn't cuddle him closer to me at that point. I watched his nose turn blue as he died.

I am left with a huge number of 'what ifs'. We both know, in our hearts, that even if he'd survived there would have been a very strong likelihood of brain damage and on-going health issues. But the one thing we had as parents was hope. We held on to that right until the very last moment.

When Adam died, so did a piece of both of us.

21st November, 2011

Cognitive Hypnotherapy. Weekend 2 of 10

On Friday night I once more jumped on a plane and headed to London for weekend number 2 of my Cognitive Hypnotherapy course.

It was a beautiful flight into London. Because I fly into London City airport, if it's a clear night you sometimes get to see all the sights of London. This was one of those nights. I saw the illuminated Houses of Parliament, St Paul's, The London Eye and the Gherkin as I flew in.

I stayed in an airport hotel once more and now it was just a short walk after landing to get there (the walk is a lot shorter once you know where you are going!). I was reading a book on the plane that had me musing on the nature of time and I'll share that with you in another post.

I've mentioned that one of the things I love so much about the course is that you learn stuff that you can use right away to help others and this weekend was no exception.

The technique we learnt this weekend is called timeline. It's nothing short of awesome. It allows you to address a problem or emotion that you want to change by going back and reprogramming your interpretation of

Nothing Needs to be the Way it's Always Been

that memory using "adult goggles". You don't lose the memory, but you change the way you respond to it. It is hugely powerful. Like many of the techniques, it works with the unconscious so is extra effective because your conscious thought process doesn't get the chance to get in the way. What's even better is that you can do the whole process without your client telling you a single thing about that memory. In fact, when we practiced with each other, all the guy I was working on would tell me was that he wanted to work on his fear of rejection. Despite that, I managed to use timeline so that it wasn't a fear for him any more.

How brilliant is that?

I really can't wait to try it on everyone. I can see what a massive difference I can make to the lives of my friends and family with this one technique. And the beauty of it is that it's a permanent change because you effectively delete all the negative associations of a memory without touching the thing itself. So there is nothing left to fire off.

So that's the good thing about the weekend – and what a big good thing it was.

You can also use timeline work to bring out a positive emotion and pull it forward to call on. We practised this one on the Saturday as a gentle introduction and to get us used to practising it before the "stronger" one on the Sunday.

This meant that over the weekend a significant proportion of our 40+ course attendees will have achieved some major steps forward in their lives!

Dawn C. Walton

I was concerned about letting someone timeline me but I figured the positive one was a safe bet to try. I chose excitement because I knew, consciously at least, I could remember times when I was excited as a child.

Good plan. However, once more I screwed up and I'm a Muppet. Now I accept failure when I'm trying something and I don't get it right at first, but failure when all I'm supposed to be doing is participating is crazy.

So we started the whole timeline thing, and then my partner took me back to have a look at the earliest memory I could find that linked to that feeling of excitement. Within seconds of looking into the black abyss that was my past I started shaking and getting upset. I opened my eyes, found an assistant to work with her and left the room.

I lost track of time, but it took me a good 15 minutes to persuade myself not to run away and to go back into the room. Trevor popped out to check on me too, which was sweet of him.

I had, and still have, no real idea what happened. Luckily I had arranged to meet Sandy after the course on the Saturday for a coffee. She patiently (I think) waited for me in the 'basement' of the local Starbucks and I'm afraid I blabbed on to her a bit because I was desperately trying to distract myself from the feeling I'd been left with. I then had a lovely dinner with Sandra so by the time I made it back to my hotel near the airport I had mostly stopped shaking but I was still confused and upset.

Nothing Needs to be the Way it's Always Been

I mailed Trevor and went in a little early on the Sunday to discuss. We agreed that I should probably have another session with him and work through it. There is something still there and I am determined to get rid of it once and for all. Yes, we are always improving ourselves and I will always have things to work on, but I want to move on from the 'big thing', whatever that may be.

I think and hope it will make me a better therapist in the long term.

Despite this, it was another brilliant weekend and I'm itching to get started so watch out, because if you come to close to me right now you are likely to get timelined!

Dawn C. Walton

24ᵗʰ November, 2011

The Battle

It's been a while since I posted anything on here about the personal journey I am on. You have been given snippets in my posts about my Cognitive Hypnotherapy course but let me give you an update.

I'm getting there but I'm not there yet!

For the first time in my life I am doing stuff that is really helping others. I am making a very tangible, positive difference in other people's lives. The high from this is beyond any drug you can take (I imagine *ahem*). It's just like a full-on adrenaline rush. Each time I do something useful, I am bouncing off the ceiling.

With happiness.

Yep, that's still there. It's the new me. The person who by default is generally a happy person (imagines smug look on Trevor's face).

I am able to appreciate so many moments in a way I have never been able to before. Moments with the little one where we spend ages laughing together. Moments with my hubby where I appreciate more than ever what an amazing person he really is and how much I love him. Moments with friends where I realise how lucky I am to have these people in my life.

Nothing Needs to be the Way it's Always Been

And I am learning.

And I love to learn. It's not just theory either, I am learning stuff I can use.

In summary, I am not useless.

And that's a bit of a revelation to me. In the same way as being happy was. I have had to shift my reality to accept this. It's very new.

I have, for most of my life, felt crap and useless so if I am no longer useless, what happens to that feeling of being a crap person?

That's where it gets interesting.

This is where the fight begins. Because the more useful I feel, the louder the "you're crap" voice shouts to compensate.

The end result of this, I'm discovering, is a full-on battle raging in my head coming out in the form of paranoia about everything I do and what everyone thinks of me and what I do.

I guess (and for the sake of illustration we'll call the 2 voices Bert and Ernie) as time passes and I do things that make me feel useful, Ernie sings his happy Rubber Ducky song and all is well with the world.

Meanwhile, Bert does not like this and is constantly nagging away to try and take the edge off that happy, useful feeling. Bert is sowing the seeds of doubt and the less he is listened to, the more he shouts and the more in Ernie's face he gets.

Dawn C. Walton

This is where I am right now. I can't remember a time where I have felt quite as paranoid and over-sensitive as I do right now.

I know it will pass. Ernie and his Rubber Ducky song will win out. I'm looking forward to that moment. Can you imagine what it will feel like to be happy, doing something that makes me feel worthwhile AND be able to accept and appreciate that because that's just who I am?

Meanwhile, I have booked another session with Trevor for January. Not only do I want to sort this, but I also want to sort out that reaction when I tried to have someone do a timeline on me (the two things may be connected of course). I want to be the best I can be and I feel that my failure to experience these different practical exercises we do fully and completely is limiting that.

Dawn C. Walton

8ᵗʰ December, 2011

The word "Step"

We know the stories, don't we?

Hansel and Gretel: The wicked stepmother doesn't think they can afford to feed them all through the winter so persuades the father (wuss!) to take his kids out to the forest and leave them there. Leaving plenty of food for the two greedy gits to scoff and two dead children. Obviously doesn't go to plan and they all live happily ever after

Cinderella: Wicked stepsisters and mother leave her scrubbing and cleaning while they live the high life. It's OK though because there's a fairy godmother who sorts it all out and they all live happily ever after

Snow White: Yet another evil stepmother who is obsessed with beauty and in the absence of plastic surgery relies on a mirror to tell her how she's looking. On discovering that her stepdaughter is prettier, goes all out to get her killed. She nearly succeeds but in the end it works out and they all live happily ever after.

Hmmm…happily ever after?

I must say that whenever I hear the word "step" with a parent I react as if they are the sort you read about in the books. Because that's how mine were. I had a

Nothing Needs to be the Way it's Always Been

stepmother and stepfather at different times in my childhood.

I get big "does not compute" words flashing in front of my eyes when I hear someone talk about a step parent with genuine fondness or even when the parent introduces themselves in that way whilst clearly talking about their child with fondness and pride.

It does not compute. For me, the fairy tales make a lot more sense.

What's interesting is that as I write this post, I started to type "and I don't believe in happily ever after".

And then I stopped.

And I thought about it.

That's what I would have written 6 months ago.

But not today.

Today, I actually believe I have entered my "happily ever after...".

Something has changed.

14th December, 2011 On a plane again…

This morning I had to fly to London again for another meeting.

The flight leaves at 8:20am from Dundee airport. The airport is only about 15 minutes from my house but I like to get there early and 'relax' while I wait for my plane, knowing that whatever happens, I am at least there and ready to fly.

Dawn C. Walton

It's a small airport with the only refreshments available once you get through security being vending machines.

"Morning, back again?" says the guy on security. He was working on Friday night when I flew down for my course.

I settle in the departures area, which is just a few seats. It's dark outside. It won't start getting light now until after 8am. I sit in silence but talk lots as I interact with the world on Twitter while I still can.

Once on the plane, everything electronic must be switched off and put away. I have my book 'Molecules of Emotion' but I'm tired and I don't like to read when we take off.

I stare out of the window and enjoy the view of the river Tay and the hills as we take off. I watch the cars on the road and try and work out which roads they are. I get frustrated that I can't share my thoughts on the view with Twitter. No electronic equipment.

Soon we pass through the clouds. Now the seat belt signs are still on but there's nothing to look at so my thoughts turn inward as they so often do.

I process all that's happened in the last few days. I think about how I've felt and why I've felt that way. I consider the steps I have taken in this personal journey I'm on. How things felt before and after my different sessions with Trevor. I think of those breakthrough moments we've had.

My thoughts then turn to our next session and the things that we need to cover. A couple of big things that

Nothing Needs to be the Way it's Always Been

have bubbled to the surface as other stuff has cleared out of the way.

And I rest there a moment. As thoughts and memories take shape. Images that run as mini video clips emerge from a fog, sharpening as they emerge. They gain 3 dimensions and then associated emotions. Each new image brings with it another. Ready to come to the fore and be heeded.

I find myself sinking emotionally as they take hold. The judgement starts and along with it a nervous, scared feeling physically makes me start to shake. Masochistically I dig deeper, search out more associations. I judge. I find myself failing against my judgement. I'm crap. I deserve nothing good. Why do I bother keeping going?

I pick up my book and read a paragraph or two. The distraction doesn't work. The voice in my head is still talking. Judging. Berating.

Then I think "I'm better than this".

"No, you're not" the voice replies.

"But I have things I've learnt now so I can deal with this myself?"

"Yeah, but you can't make them work on yourself, can you?" the voice replies.

I stare out of the window and watch another plane cross our path way above us. The jets of the engines leaving a trail behind.

I think through all I have learnt.

Dawn C. Walton

And I remember dropthrough. That I learnt this weekend and that worked on me.

"I'm gonna try it,

"I think.

I close my eyes.

What's the first emotion?

Fear.

OK drop through it to below. Now what would you call that?

Afraid.

Hmm that's the same thing, isn't it? I'm failing, aren't I? But it's not. Afraid feels different than fear.

I keep going.

I find 'pathetic' again. Seems to appear a lot, that one.

But very quickly I have passed through all the negative feelings. I'm in the holding space at the end of negative. I know if I keep going I'll get to the good feelings. I enjoy chilling for a moment. I rest on a cloud.

Then I keep going.

What's below that?

Happy.

I smile. I feel calm. I've done it.

I'm like a little puppy, I want to email Trevor and tell him I did it so he can pat me on the head and say well

Nothing Needs to be the Way it's Always Been

done! No electronic equipment. It's good. I pester him too much. I really should be able to do this stuff on my own now anyway.

So I write this post and share it with all of you.

People come to the Cognitive Hypnotherapy course at the Quest Institute for all sorts of different reasons. Not all want to set up as therapists. A lot are on it to improve themselves.

Today, I understand how powerful it is for that.

Dawn C. Walton

19ᵗʰ December, 2011

Thinking Slimmer 31 weeks

To be honest, I've kind of lost track of time here. It's about 7.5 months that I've been doing Thinking Slimmer, I think. The last 6 months have been such a whirlwind. So much has changed in my life.

Mentally I've been struggling the last month or so. I continue to listen to my Slimpod. I now listen to the "Drop 2 Jeans sizes" which initially I didn't like but I've got used to it now and think it works better for me. My eating habits remain the same. I kept a food log for a week recently and it showed that I eat very little but there is a lot more to do on what I eat.

Having 'gone off' Diet Coke, I am also finding it a challenge to drink enough. I don't like water or squash. I have started drinking sparkling water with a bit of fresh orange juice but still not enough. Something else to work on.

Meanwhile, despite buying and fitting into a new size 14 jumper, I still look at myself and see a very overweight person. I can stand in the mirror in my size 14 jeans that now need a belt to stay up and my size 14 top and see that I have so far to go. The weight is starting to go off the scales again after a 'blip' where I had to stop weighing before I went mad. So I am now around

Nothing Needs to be the Way it's Always Been

12 stone. Down from 16 stone-ish. I am now a size 14. Down from a 20/22. And I feel really, really fat. All I can see when I look in the mirror is how fat I am. One day I will look in the mirror and not see a fat person. But I still have some way to go.

Now for the other big news...

...are you ready?

...really?

Well, I was approached by a PR company to see if I would be interested in running the London Marathon in 2012 on behalf of their client. The offer includes a training plan and support, kit, tickets etc.

I said yes.

Yep, you read that right.

Me. Who hates running yet still runs most days.

Me. Who can't run but so far has run as far as 8.3 miles.

Me. Who struggles to find time for work, being a mum and doing my course.

Me. I'm going to run the London Marathon in 2012.

Me. I'm off my trolley!

I guess with the training plan I'm going to need to follow, it will be impossible not to get to my target size by April 22nd next year. This is the date of the marathon.

20th December, 2011

The London Marathon and me

So in a previous post I told you that I have signed up to do the London Marathon in 2012. For many years I have watched it on the TV, wondering what it would be like to take part, but never seriously considering that I would. After all, I'm not a runner.

If you've been following this blog for a while you will know I've been running for the last few months.

You will also know I don't particularly like running. I do it for two reasons:

1. It's the only form of exercise I can't find an excuse to get out of. You can run anywhere.

2. I need the fresh air to choose my mood each day. The endorphins I get from running have been a significant contributor to my progress towards happiness.

I do not see myself as a runner.

I now run Mon-Fri as long as it's practical to do so (i.e. I am not away with work).

I have been doing a longer run on a Sunday for quite a while. The furthest I have ever run is 8.3 miles. I was really trying for 10 miles until I got an awful cold and

Nothing Needs to be the Way it's Always Been

did my foot in. The reason I was trying for 10 miles is because Trevor, Becca and Darin were doing the Great South Run. Becca and Darin are people I have connected with through Thinking Slimmer. Although I wasn't going, I wanted to prove to myself I could do the distance. But for the first time I had the thought that maybe it would be good to do a 'race' so that I had something to aim for.

The 8.3 miles showed me that I could probably manage a half-marathon.

So I looked for something local. Between work and my course it's just not practical for me to travel to do a run. Besides, it's a big ask for someone who only runs for leisure to travel to an unknown city to take part in a race.

It seemed I had just missed every key local race.

So I settled down to the day-to-day challenges of running. It was now too dark before I started work in the morning to have a run. I was looking at the treadmill with hatred. It doesn't meet the criteria for point 2 of why I run.

But once the frost and ice arrived then I had no choice. It is not even thawing through the day right now. I can neither cycle nor run safely at this time of year, it seems. So I started running on the treadmill. I was doing short runs and concentrating on going as fast as I could. I was doing 10-minute miles. Our treadmill seems to crash if you swap pace too often – so interval training would have been ideal but wasn't possible.

Then I got an email. From Nestle Pure Life – the official water sponsor of the London Marathon – asking if I would be interested in being sponsored by them to run it in 2012. I knew Becca was doing it. My first thought was "how cool would that be as an achievement in life".

My second thought was "arghhhhhhhhhh".

They provide support through FullPotential who run training days and write a training plan just for you. They provide gear and tickets for friends and family to come and see you finish. And it just seemed like a once in a lifetime opportunity that I had to take.

My biggest worry is not the marathon itself. I know that I can do anything I put my mind to. Even if I had to walk it, I would get round. My worry is the time to train. I figure I can run before work in the morning. But as the runs get longer – it's harder. It took me an hour to run 5 miles on Sunday. The little one gets me up at 7 so most of the time I should be OK. The longest runs happen closer to the April 22nd date anyway.

The Sunday long runs will be tough. When we get to 10+ miles we are talking between 2 and 3 hours of running. I am hoping that I can call on my friend to look after the little one on a Sunday afternoon while I have a run.

Of course, I will be away with work occasionally, and I am on my course 1 weekend a month but hoping to use the gym at the college.

It is only 4 months. 4 months of training. I can adapt. I will do my best and that's all I can do.

So I said yes.

Nothing Needs to be the Way it's Always Been

Next year could potentially be one of the most amazing years of my life so far.

1. I will turn 40 in October.

2. Having already lost 4 stone, it is likely that I will lose the remaining weight and reach my target size.

3. I will be qualified as a Cognitive Hypnotherapist and start my new career.

4. I will continue to be happy in life and, by then, I will be happy and comfortable with myself.

5. I will have completed the London Marathon. Something I never dreamed I would do.

It appears that where 2007 was the year that changed my life in all the wrong ways, 2012 will be the year that changes my life in all the right ways.

And I just want to note, for the record, how lucky I am to have such an amazing husband who supports me in everything I do, as I try and build a better life for all of us. I love him more than anything.

Dawn C. Walton

23rd December, 2011

In 2012...

On the Cognitive Hypnotherapy forum there was a thread started that I really like the idea of.

It's called a future pace.

The idea is that you write a post as if it's December 2012 and the year has passed. You are reflecting on your achievements and challenges of the year. I think it's a great idea.

It is particularly interesting for me.

If you'd asked me 6 months ago I could not have even thought of tomorrow, let alone next year. Now I can look right out to 2012 and beyond. So this was my response. What would yours be?

In 2012...

...I ran the London Marathon. Amazing myself that I wasn't the last person to cross the finishing line and that I crossed it the same day as I crossed the start line.

I passed my Cognitive Hypnotherapy course and immediately went into business part time generating a steady and reasonable income from weekend and evening work.

Nothing **Needs to be the Way it's Always Been**

I spent the year feeling happy for the first time in my life and looking forward to the future. Over time, I was able to help the hubby feel happy too (let's face it, it would be very annoying being around me otherwise).

The little one started full time school and loved every minute. She complains all the time when she can't go to school at the weekend!

I reached my target weight and still get a buzz from going into a clothes shop and choosing based on what I like rather than what fits.

I turned 40.

2012 was the best year of my entire life. Without doubt (with a leader to make it that way from 2011).

So you want a turn? What happened in 2012 for you?

Dawn C. Walton

29ᵗʰ December, 2011

Reflections from 2011 into 2012

Last year I blogged about the year ahead. I was
remarkably optimistic I thought! But I liked the way it
worked out so will do the same for this year.

What can I say about the year that's just passed?
For once I'm not thinking "good riddance, at last"
I'm actually planning for the year ahead
I'm not dreading the days, I'm excited instead

So what's driven such a big change in my thinking?
Have I taken drugs or done some heavy drinking?
The answer is 'no' the reason is more legal
I've had my life changed by some amazing people.

Let's start with a lady called Sandra who's become quite
a mate
After she came into my life to help me lose some weight
With nothing more than listening for 10 mins a day
To a guy called Trevor who talks reassuringly away

So far I've lost four sizes and four stone
I've chucked six bags of clothes cos it won't go back on
I've signed up to run the 2012 London Marathon
Because my Slimpod made me think "I'll go for a run!"

Nothing Needs to be the Way it's Always Been

Which leads me to the next person who totally
changed me
An amazing man called Trevor who I first went to see
When Sandra suggested he could help me move on
And finally resolve issues I'd been running away from

I didn't really believe that he could live up to what
she said
How could anyone ever fix the mess in my head?
But with patience and genius this amazing man
showed me
That despite everything that's happened, I can be happy!

Work still sucks and I still have problems with my boss
But in my new frame of mind I see it's the company's loss
Because now I am training for a brand new career
And I'll be moving on from my job by the end of the year

My daughter is now just about 3 and a half
And a day doesn't pass where she doesn't make us laugh
She now goes to pre-school for 2.5 hours a day
She thrives around other kids where she can learn
and play

We got on top of her gluten intolerance
Despite some incidents that happened more than once
But I bake her cookies and cake and fresh bread
We've got "check for wheat" ingrained in her head!

She's so bright and funny she lights up our world
She's such an amazing and beautiful girl

Dawn C. Walton

We still can't believe how lucky we are
She's the best thing I've done in my life by far

My hubby's best friend died earlier this year
Close to Adam's birthday, meaning we both shed
many tears
We also decided that we wouldn't move for now
With his friend passed on the desire was gone somehow

I managed to write over 60,000 words of my book
And send it out to a few publishers to have a look
It also meant I got my first rejection letter
But I've not lost heart, I'll keep making it better

And one day I will get my novel printed
And maybe sell film rights and become totally minted!
By the end of the year I'll be changing the lives all the time
Of many people, in the way Trevor changed mine.

So bring on 2012, the best year yet
Thanks to the amazing people I've met
And with my wonderful hubby and little one too,
I'll be using this blog to share it all with you!

Dawn C. Walton

3ʳᵈ January, 2012

On reflection

There is so much going on in my head right now. Not unusual for me, I guess. Also not a coincidence given I am seeing Trevor again a week on Friday.

There is an inevitable stirring up of feelings before a session that I am starting to accept now.

So why another session? Before Xmas we had 3 sessions. 2 of them were very intense. Those of you following my journey, or indeed just chatting to me over the last year or so, have observed a huge difference.

I have become a positive and happy person. So to all intents and purposes, things are looking rosy. I am running the London Marathon - a once in a lifetime opportunity. I am taking control of my life and choosing to do things for me, to make me and my family happier. This is a first for me. Before I didn't care about my future. In fact, I didn't want it.

So why did I book another session with Trevor?

Because I'm waiting for the bubble to burst. I am waiting for the consequences of this happiness to hit me and I really don't expect them to be good. Because you see, someone like me doesn't deserve any of this.

Nothing Needs to be the Way it's Always Been

Now as I read books and as I attend my cognitive hypnotherapy course, and even as Trevor and others show me that it doesn't have to be this way, I know that by now I should be able to break out of this way of thinking.

I should.

And Trevor says we are all fellow strugglers and he is so right. I see now how we are all struggling in some way and I am particularly thrilled that I'm learning how to help others. There are many of you who say you've been inspired by my journey. I'm very happy about that but I don't understand it.

I can't argue with your reality but I fail to see how you could possibly be inspired by someone like me.

And so I have booked another session with Trevor. Because I know he has helped me achieve so much already. Once more I have failed to move forward on my own. For now, that just stacks up against all the other things I feel like a failure at.

Because at the end of the day, right at this moment, I don't feel like I deserve all this wonderful stuff I'm now experiencing. Every time someone says I inspire them, I feel like a fraud - like I am misleading them somehow. Every time someone says I deserve this happiness, I feel I have cheated them.

I should be better than this. I should treat this as a voice and tell it to shut up. I should practise what I've learnt.

Dawn C. Walton

But I can't and that makes me feel so useless, almost to the point of embarrassment.

So a week on Friday, Trevor will help me - again. And maybe this last significant thing will allow me to move on and truly appreciate what I have.

Dawn C. Walton

10ᵗʰ January, 2012

But now it's different...

It is Tuesday.

...time is ticking on. On Friday I see Trevor again for another session. One that I didn't expect to need and as time ticks on, other things come to the surface that need addressing. Now that the noise has gone. Now that things have changed so very much.

As the last 6 months have passed there have been so many changes that even I don't recognise the person I am now. And sometimes, it is worth pausing time for a moment and reflecting on what some of those changes are:

1. I used to hate the passing of time. I honestly didn't want to make it to the next hour, let alone the next day or week. I used to try and think about ambitions etc but I couldn't see my future. I didn't want to see my future. Not being melodramatic. I am being factual. Despite my lovely husband and daughter, living with me, every minute of every day seemed like torture...

...But now it's different. I am excited about my future. I have plans in my head that cover the next few years. I no longer live in the moment but live for the moments

Nothing Needs to be the Way it's Always Been

that are to come because I know how exciting they will be. I love living my life with all its potential

2. There was a constant noise in my head. "I hate you" it said. Again and again. Every few seconds. I would look out on the world through my eyes but it was like there was someone else in my head really driving me. And that someone said "I hate you", "you are worthless", "why do you even bother?" And I was used to living my life in such a way as I didn't listen. I ignored that voice for everything. I was an actress in my life, playing the role but never feeling or living my life. Time was passing and I was surviving…

…But now it's different. The noise has gone. I look on the world through my own eyes and live my life as me and not as an actress. I feel everything and am part of everything that happens. I no longer have to think "how should I respond, how should I act, what would be normal?" but trust in myself.

3. I used to be scared of emotions. I was scared that if I genuinely experienced anything, then I would totally lose control of my mind. The only way to function was to not feel…

…But now it's different. My emotions have been unlocked and now I can feel in a way that I have never experienced before. I have learnt that I can feel without losing control. That means that for the first time in my life I have felt genuinely happy. In fact, I can safely say that my default state is happy and chilled with the normal daily bad moments interspersed. This is quite the turnaround. I am even getting accused of being positive these days. Bizarre!

4. I used to obsess about my past. I was constantly looking for answers or explanations. Why me? What was it about me? Every contact I had with anyone or anything from my past turned me upside down. I even had my father on my Facebook because I desperately wanted him to give me some answers…

…But now it's different. I don't care. My past is a story without the associated emotions. I removed my father from my Facebook within weeks of seeing Trevor for the first time. I didn't need answers any more. And I certainly didn't need him in my life. There are still twinges and shadows. There are things I resent and am angry about. But you know what, that is a good thing. Anger means I no longer blame myself and that is how it should be.

So this is where I am.

Is it really possible for so much to change in such a short space of time? It seems so.

And maybe it's because it has all happened so quickly that I am struggling right now to believe that I deserve this. I am waiting for the world to come crashing down around my ears and once more to put me in my place. "Don't dare to dream. Don't dare to be happy. This is not what was meant for you in your life".

And that shows me that there is still something to work on here.

Nothing Needs to be the Way it's Always Been

So on Friday we will work on that. And maybe I can learn to appreciate being me. And maybe I can stop feeling like such a failure at everything I do. Maybe I can stop feeling like such a fraud when someone says I inspired them to do something. Maybe I can look to my future without those expectations of the catastrophic event happening to screw everything up.

Let's face it, if anyone can help me make this change it's Trevor. So roll on Friday and session number 4.

5 - Session 4

15th January, 2012

Weekend 4, day 2 – subcon is still a git

So I told you how this weekend was all about the healing aspects of Cognitive Hypnotherapy. It was fascinating and day 2 lived up to the expectations set by a great day 1.

But first let me give you a little context to my mindset.

You should be aware that I went for another session with Trevor on Friday. The way these work is that he usually does 'stuff' that has an immediate effect, but then early the week after he sends me a Wordweaving recording that he has done for me that I can listen to daily to reinforce the things that we covered (similar to the slimpods but specific to me and my issues).

I usually have about a week of turmoil as I try and adapt to the change in my mindset from the work we've done together. There are such significant shifts in a way of thinking that I've held for over 20 years that it really throws me at first.

So the 'stuff' on Friday was truly amazing. It felt like someone had lifted a huge weight from me. When I say 'huge', I visualised it as an anvil being lifted off my chest. The effect was immediate as I walked out of the room filled with an unfamiliar sense of calm and confidence.

Nothing Needs to be the Way it's Always Been

I then met with different people and went straight into day 1 of my course, not getting a chance to really process anything until I headed to Watford yesterday evening.

In the meantime, the change in me was also noticeable on the course (even Trevor noticed it). Unlike before I felt comfortable with my level of skills and knowledge. I have put a lot of time into this because it is something I believe in so much. As you will know if you've been reading this blog for a while, I truly believe I have found my 'thing' in life. In previous courses when people have commented on all the work I've done practising and my participation in the forum discussions, I have cringed and felt bad over it. This weekend I felt good about what I know. I was happy to discuss with my fellow course attendees. I was accepting of observations as a compliment and not a criticism.

On top of that, this weekend confirmed that the last 3 people I have used my new-found skills to help have all benefited to varying degrees from that help. In other words, it worked.

So I enjoyed this weekend more than any other (and that's saying something) because I could participate openly and with confidence. When my subconscious was a git yesterday, I didn't make it an "oh woe is me" moment. I didn't even regard it as me failing on the exercise - I just decided my subcon was a git!

Of course, today it proved that again. My subcon and me are going to have to have some serious words. A lot of the things we do involve visualisations. I think I've mentioned in a previous blog post, the best way to work

Dawn C. Walton

with concepts like feelings is to first try and make a tangible representation of the them that you can alter in some way. This is more so with healing than anything else. We are making use of the fact that the mind and body are one interconnected organism, so if you work with the mind, then by default you are working with the body too.

One such exercise involves the therapist and client sharing their resources for this healing in a way that utilises a physical connection between the two of them, combined with a visualisation, to achieve a healing in some area. Usually this is done by clasping a hand together with the other person. The one receiving the healing then visualises, with guidance, how that physical connection may act as a conduit to help the healing flow into their body (if you don't believe in the strength of connection between the mind and the body you should probably skip this post!).

Believe it or not, I am perfectly fit and healthy. I really struggled to find something that I would like healing. But I am up for everything and given the brattish behaviour of my subcon yesterday, I figured I'd have another bash at the whole skin thing. Now I love visualisations. I am a very visual person and I find other people's visualisations really interesting. But I just couldn't grasp it. As time went on, the skin thing wasn't working and I started getting a pain in my shoulder. My shoulder is fine. I have no complaints about my shoulder. Or should I say 'had'! We ended the exercise and I had a real pain in my shoulder. Not from the angle I was holding it at for the exercise either (before you

Nothing Needs to be the Way it's Always Been

say that). Very bizarre. It's OK because we learnt more techniques that helped me get over it (including one named after Dr Angel Escudero that has been used many times for people to stay fully conscious during operations with the critical areas being anaesthetised by them - Google it, it's amazing!).

So either I do have a problem there and it was being brought to light, or, as I prefer to think, my subcon is a git!

Anyway, all in all a brilliant weekend, which has now expanded my toolkit even further to be able to help even more people improve their lives. Trevor was also on particularly good form, so not only did we all learn loads, but we had a right good laugh at the same time.

Apart from the practicalities of travel etc, I don't ever want this course to end. It is the best thing I've ever learnt in my life. So form an orderly queue, because as each month passes I am learning to do more and more so that pretty soon I will be able to have a bash at helping anyone with anything.

Dawn C. Walton

18ᵗʰ January, 2012

Unburdened

It is very strange to find myself writing this so soon after a session with Trevor.

In previous sessions we have done 'stuff' and although it has had an immediate, often dramatic, impact, it has taken a good few weeks for my head and my emotions to catch up with each other and settle. To understand what this new way of thinking means to the way I interact with the world.

It is not an easy process. Not at all. There is lots of confusion and turmoil. There are moments of insight and clarity but also some real lows.

But that is inevitable. After all, we are reprogramming more than 20 years of beliefs and behaviours and that doesn't change overnight.

Well, it didn't previously, anyway.

But this one was different and I'm not really sure why.

After this session I felt like I had been relieved of a massive burden I was carrying around. I walked out of the room feeling free in a way I've never felt before.

And this was a feeling. My head still hadn't caught up with what we did. It still hasn't.

Nothing Needs to be the Way it's Always Been

For the first time I am being governed by the feeling as opposed to the thoughts. The old thoughts remain but find no response when they are triggered.

I attended my course at the weekend feeling calm and relaxed and almost self-assured. My head kept on saying "what the hell is going on here"!

It is an amazing feeling. I am going into situations or even thoughts with expectations of how it will make me feel that are no longer true.

If I thought I was happy before, I was miles off. This is what it's all about. This is the Dawn I was always supposed to be.

"The best is yet to come" is something Trevor keeps telling me. After Friday I reckon we're getting pretty darned close, to be honest.

In an email the other day, Trevor made what seemed like a throwaway comment but, knowing him, was probably just another nudge against my boundaries. We were talking about what all these childhood experiences are that we're sorting in the context of what I share with you on this blog.

"Most people reading will guess what it's about".

And you know what, maybe as you've been reading you have an inkling. But that is all. You don't know what it's all about. And maybe one day I'll tell you (that I can write that shows how far I've come). But the first 18 years of my life were a write-off for many different reasons.

A few years back, the hubby and I looked into fostering. We both wanted to give other kids a chance to have at least some part of their childhood that was safe, nurturing and loving. That's why we wanted to foster, not adopt.

We went all the way through the process, 12 weeks of training etc. But the social services people didn't like the idea that I was out working and the hubby was at home. Despite have a solid base, large house, garden, 1 parent at home at all times, willingness etc. In the end their determination paid off and we never submitted the final form.

The point to the story? In one training session we covered the different ways children may be abused. On a reasonably long list, there was only 1 thing I couldn't put a tick against applying to me.

But it doesn't matter, does it? Because thanks to Trevor and Cognitive Hypnotherapy, none of that matters any more. It no longer defines me. What it does do is give me the resources I need to be the best Cognitive Hypnotherapist I can possibly be. Because now, I can use that to help as many people as possible. And if I only achieve for them a fraction of what Trevor has done for me, then it makes it all worthwhile.

Without my past I would not be at this point now. And this is one of the coolest places to be. It's so good, that I want you all to hang out here with me.

So I'm going to say something now I never thought I'd say. I'm grateful for my childhood. For everything that happened. For what I have learnt. Because it brought me to Trevor and the beginning of what is going to be a truly amazing future.

23rd January, 2012

Into the wardrobe

This is my attempt to use Narnia to explain where I am on my personal journey. Bear with me on this one, and if you have never read The Chronicles Of Narnia I suggest you skip this post!

One day you step into a room that has always been there but you were never aware of. A set of circumstances came together such that one day, you find yourself walking into that room. *For me, those circumstances were talking to Sandra at Thinking Slimmer about why I felt it wouldn't work for me.*

In that room you spot a wardrobe. It is big and intimidating, but you look behind you and where you have come from is far worse. You take a deep breath and walk into the wardrobe. At first it is dark and weird, but you discover you can keep walking through the wardrobe. You push through even though it is scary but where you have come from is worse. Eventually you discover that the wardrobe leads to a new, unfamiliar world that is both different and exciting. *Stepping through the wardrobe was making the decision to go and see Trevor, the founder of Cognitive Hypnotherapy.*

This new world shows you that the place you have come from is not the only way the world has to be. There are

Nothing Needs to be the Way it's Always Been

other worlds and other ways of living. You meet new and different people who don't know anything about where you have come from and treat you as the person you present, and judge you by the behaviours you exhibit instead of the "why" behind the way you are. You find it liberating to see that you can be who you choose to be.

You keep glancing back to the where the wardrobe is, and wondering if you should go back. Sometimes you even try it but it's as if, now you have seen that there is a different world out there, this old place is twice as scary. You realise you like being whoever you choose to be.

Then one day you meet Aslan. He teaches you how to tap into your resources. He guides you through the challenges you face day-by-day, to draw on those resources instead of assuming you were defined by where you came from. He teaches you that nothing needs to be now the way it used to be before. *This is Trevor.*

There are days where you struggle. You find you need to constantly draw on Aslan's guidance over what to do as you are faced with new and unfamiliar situations. Even when not with him, his words echo in your head as you explore what your resources are.

Increasingly you are faced with situations where your new friends come to you for your help. You give it willingly, happy to share in a way you have never been able to before. Thrilled that you can help. There are battles and challenges in this new world, and soon you realise that the lessons you have learnt have given you the strength to lead others through those battles.

Dawn C. Walton

You find, over time, you think about the wardrobe less and less.

You find, over time, that you are far more defined by your new behaviours than anything you brought with you from the other world.

And you find, over time, that you no longer seek out Aslan for guidance constantly. You look forward to seeing him but treat his company more as that of a friend than a guide. Appreciating him for his own qualities rather than the lessons you need to learn from him.

One day, as you are out riding, you come across an area of your new world that is familiar. You vaguely recollect that it has meaning but you also remember that it was not a good place to go back to.

Smiling to yourself, you turn away from that place and carry on living your life, surrounded by people you love and living your life the way you choose to live it.

Dawn C. Walton

2nd February, 2012

Everything changes

I don't know me any more.

I've never been here before.

I don't know where I'm going and yet I'm excited.

Who I am is changing daily and I love it.

Dawn C. Walton

6th February, 2012

It seems that it is human nature to focus on those things in our day that do not go as we would like, rather than accept and enjoy the successes we have.

When we are trying to drive some kind of change in our lives, the success of that change can be very dependent on our ability to acknowledge progress and forgive failure.

Let's face it, there are very few fundamental life changes that happen overnight (certainly not the good sort anyway!).

So how do we rise out of the darkness and choose to make our lives positive? How do we take control ourselves, of the way things go, and choose to interpret things in the most positive way possible?

...and more importantly, what the heck am I doing writing this post?!

Those of you who have been following this blog for a while will know that when I first started my Cognitive Hypnotherapy, one of the things I was asked to do after my first session was to review the positive(s) in my day at the end of each day.

This is not something that has ever come naturally to me.

I have chosen the stance of a pessimist in life. Expect the worst, then you can't be disappointed. Expect the worst

203

Nothing Needs to be the Way it's Always Been

and things will almost always turn out better than you expect.

But it's not a great approach for recognising change. Especially when you are trying to reprogramme the way you have thought for 20 years. Or when you are trying to lose weight and you just want it to be gone and for everything to be different.

So I set about blogging my positive of the day. It's fair to say I didn't get it quite right because I was picking big things each day. Then again, big things were happening to me.

But it did help me to learn to focus on what was changing instead of what was not. It tuned me in to a certain way of thinking that I have continued since then.

Now, I am very clued up to things that are different in me, and this is still often a daily insight (even though I don't blog it daily any more). It also helps me with my Thinking Slimmer journey as despite not feeling like I'm losing weight, I am able to focus on the signs that I am different now.

I still haven't learnt to forgive myself for my 'failures'. I am hoping that one day I will become as good at that as I am now at recognising my achievements.

What do you think? Worth a bash.

At the end of each day, take a moment and write it down (if you love notepads, buy a shiny one for this), or blog it, or even put it in your mobile phone each day in your calendar. Imagine how much fun it will be to look back after a few months and review your Positive of the Day.

Dawn C. Walton

7th February, 2012

My brother

Let me tell you about my brother

This is obviously very sketchy in some of the details.

My mother was born with a form of Spina Bifida that meant she had a hole in her spine. The problems she suffered as a child were put down to growing pains but when she gave birth to me and my brother, who is nearly 2 years older than me, they realised there was something serious going on.

When I was about 3 my mother ended up in hospital because of this.

At some point during her time in hospital my father got together with my stepmother. She moved in and my mother was kicked out.

My brother and I lived with my father and stepmother until I was about 9. She didn't like us. We were neglected and hit often. It wasn't fun. We saw my mother very little. In fact, the first time I saw her after the split I didn't know who she was.

As we got older, my mother met a new man who would later become my stepfather. We went to stay with them occasionally.

Nothing Needs to be the Way it's Always Been

Then one year, when I was about 9, we went to stay with them and we never went back. From that point onwards we lived with my mother and my stepfather.

My brother and I could have been united by the experiences of our early years but we were not. He disliked me and used to threaten to punch me many thousands of times (typical kid stuff) if I did something he didn't like or spoke when he didn't want me to. We didn't share toys. If we went anywhere together I had to walk some way behind him. To him I was never anything more than an annoying sister that he didn't want around.

When we moved in with our mother, we lived as separate lives as is possible at that age. My father disowned us and didn't have anything further to do with us. In later years, my brother would visit him and they would chat. If I tried to visit him, I was sent packing sharpish.

Life was no better living with my stepfather and mother. My mother was ill and limited, and my stepfather was a bastard.

Still, my brother and I never really pulled together to support each other.

We moved back to Wales when I was 10 or so and life carried on as it had always done. Then, shortly before his 16th birthday my brother ran away from home, down to London. My parents went to get him and brought him back.

Dawn C. Walton

But now he had learnt what he needed to do. He waited until after his 16th birthday and ran away again. This time they didn't bring him back.

I never forgave him for running away and leaving me. Given our relationship, there was no way he would have taken me with him, but I always wished he had.

He stayed in touch with my mother occasionally and every now and then he would visit. He had a tough time. He always wanted to be a punk and has been ever since he left home. He has been on drugs since then and has had a few close shaves, for sure. But he is one of life's survivors and no matter what happens, he always seems to come through OK.

A good number of years ago, he got in touch with me. He said family was the most important thing and he tried to reconnect. I have tried for many years to accept that connection, but family isn't important to me, and he abandoned me, leaving me to deal with everything on my own.

A few years back I went to his wedding. It was unique and I made a unique cake to go with it.

I have a wonderful family and an amazing life now.

I have also found acceptance of myself and learnt to be happy in my life.

One day, I might try and help him do the same thing.

Dawn C. Walton

9th February, 2012

Feel the fear and do it anyway

It's now been 4 weeks since my last session with Trevor.

These days I am way better at being tuned into the differences in myself after these sessions but, to be honest, it would be impossible not to notice this time.

My school report when I was about 16 read "does well in familiar surroundings". The 'best' category was worded as "does well in familiar and unfamiliar surroundings".

I was always put out by not getting the best score but the reality is that it was a very accurate assessment.

You see, I have always been scared of everything. So much so that I have always had to ignore what my head is saying (Run away and hide!) in order to function effectively. If going somewhere new, I would always do a check to make sure I had worked out where the front door was, (if possible)!

Take a deep breath, close your eyes and jump.

That has been my mantra for life. Don't let your doubts dictate your behaviours. For me, that was the only way I could ever do anything.

But it didn't change the fact that every situation with an element of something new was terrifying to me and required me to draw on my inner resources to do it.

209

Nothing Needs to be the Way it's Always Been

Last week I took a trip to Enniskillen with work.
For a trip like this I would check I had all the travel
arrangements sorted. I had to hire a car and drive after
flying, so I would have printed the map. I would have
the contact details of the hotel. I would be incredibly
nervous until I reached my hotel.

But it was different.

I wasn't nervous. I was actually excited.

I felt like a kid seeing a whole new world.

"I'm different," I thought.

"I don't recognise this person."

You see, it seems I am no longer scared of everything.

I don't get drowned in a feeling of dread.

I no longer have to 'Feel the fear and do it anyway'.

I hadn't realised how much that fear dictated so many
dimensions of my daily life. I only realised when it
was gone.

So there you go, the latest change from my sessions with
Trevor is that I am no longer scared of everything.

Pretty cool.

Dawn C. Walton

12ᵗʰ February, 2012

Weekend 5 – Day 2

Well where do I start?

After the course yesterday a few us went to the pub for dinner. And as I mentioned in yesterday's post, I decided, in a moment of temporary insanity, to try and meet up with my brother. The logistics of this required me to book and pay for a cab for him to come over to my hotel, and the same in return.

He lives in New Cross and there was no way I was going there!

It was after 10pm by the time he arrived and it was about 1:30am when I waved goodbye to him. I got him to record a video for the little one which he did in his own inimitable way and scared the heck out of her when she watched it! At least it gives her time to get used to him before she meets him in person when I bring her down with me to watch me run the marathon.

I wanted to suss out what I could do for him using Cognitive Hypnotherapy. My conclusion was 'not a lot'. Firstly he was very much 'I see how it can work for some but it won't for me'. It took all my skills to explain it to him and I eventually had to break out the pendulum to prove it. He also has epilepsy and hears voices as a result

Nothing Needs to be the Way it's Always Been

of the way he's abused his body with drugs and alcohol over the years. Neither of these are particularly good around hypnotherapy. I think if anyone can help him, it will have to be one of my fellow trainees at Quest. He would be great practice for them, though!

It appears he spent 6 weeks over xmas in prison. How he has got to 41, having been a junkie since he was 16, without a previous record is a mystery - but he has. It apparently was a huge fear for him and he took some pretty drastic steps to avoid going in there. But it seems, that once there, he coped well and his biggest problem was a horrible purple tracksuit they made him wear. At least he still had his tattoos!

He headed home in a taxi at 1:30am - with all the money I had in my wallet to keep him going and a bottle of Magners in his pocket!

Needless to say, I didn't sleep well and it was well past 2am before I settled. I was up again at 5am. I don't cope well with contact with certain members of my family and I feel like I have taken a number of steps back after meeting him. I have spent the day either wanting to cry or run headlong into the nearest wall multiple times. I don't entirely understand why I feel this way but I'm sure it will pass because of that. If it was more solid I could use a technique. The fact that it isn't must mean it will pass (I hope!).

At least it wasn't too cold this morning. I even managed a chat with this little chappy on the way home.

So on the course: this weekend is, I think, one of the most powerful weekends for the personal development

Dawn C. Walton

of the people on the course. We look initially at what our values are in life, usually around either our relationships or our careers. The way these exercises work is that you first list all your values, then you rank them in priority (usually surprising yourself by the ones that come top) and then you get to the "what's that all about?" of each of the values to get to the real underlying drivers.

You know how we often say "there's part of me that wants to X" or something like that? Well, we look at the limiting belief we have around these values. Then we do one of the coolest techniques in the Cognitive Hypnotherapy toolkit called Visual Squash

In this technique you visualise the two different parts of yourself on each hand. You do some work to show that actually both the part you want to resolve and the other, often more positive, part have the same intention in your subconscious. Then with your eyes closed your hands come together and in that the two parts become integrated.

It was very powerful for many people on the course, including my partner who said it was the biggest and most significant change in her since we started the course. It was nice to have been in a position to make that possible.

So now I am once more waiting in London City Airport. My friend was up for the weekend and has now gone home. She had a fab day with the little one yesterday, taking her all over the place. This morning the little one

Nothing Needs to be the Way it's Always Been

wasn't well and actually had a nap, which is unheard of. But apparently she perked up after, so fingers crossed.

I am sure this feeling I am carrying will pass soon, and I'm sure having only 3 hours sleep has something to do with it! Luckily I am off work Friday - Tuesday next week so might get a chance to catch up with myself!

Dawn C. Walton

14ᵗʰ February, 2012

Quantum leap and me

I used to love Quantum Leap the TV series. This is the Wiki write up:

Quantum Leap is an American television series that was broadcast on NBC from March 26, 1989 to May 5, 1993, for a total of five seasons. The series was created by Donald Bellisario, and starred Scott Bakula as Dr. Sam Beckett, a physicist from six years in the future (during the series' original run) who becomes lost in time following a time travel experiment, temporarily taking the places of other people to "put right what once went wrong". Dean Stockwell co-starred as Al Calavicci, Sam's womanizing, cigar-smoking sidekick and best friend, who appeared as a hologram that only Sam, animals, and young children could see and hear. The series featured a mix of comedy, drama and melodrama, social commentary, nostalgia and science fiction, which won it a broad range of fans. One of its trademarks is that at the end of each episode, Sam "leaps" into the setting for the next episode, usually uttering a dismayed "Oh, boy!"

It occurred to me, as I have struggled since meeting with my brother, that it is awfully like a Quantum Leap scenario.

In the programme, Sam, the main character, gets dragged back through time and finds himself in a

Nothing Needs to be the Way it's Always Been

scenario in someone else's body. It takes him a while to work out who he is. He then has to become that person whilst using his own innate skills to solve their problem so he can leap back out of their body again.

I thought I had reached a point in my personal journey where I was pretty much sorted.

I feel happy, confident and in control. I look at each day and each week with optimism. I enjoy my life and sharing it with the people around me. On Saturday, as I sat giggling at Trevor as he taught the course I realised that I was looking at him almost as a stranger. He was the bloke teaching the course and not so much the bloke who helped me change my life. It was actually quite bizarre!

Then on Saturday night I met with my brother. I paid for a taxi to bring him to my hotel and to take him back home again.

I stayed up until 1:30am talking to him. I was trying to work out if I could help and I realised I couldn't. Maybe someone else can but not me. He told me about all his troubles. He told me how he'd tried to kill himself and put his affairs in order, written a will etc. Apparently I was named in it but what he has that I'd want I have no idea! He told me how he didn't plan on living much beyond the next 2-3 years. He told me that he was chilled and contented right now and then without realising it shared with me that it clearly wasn't true.

I talked to him about Cognitive Hypnotherapy. He said he understood how it worked but it wouldn't work on him. But I could tell he would like it to. I used the

Dawn C. Walton

pendulum on him and he realised how powerful it was but he couldn't think of anything he'd like to ask it to change.

I told him I was happy. He didn't even acknowledge what I said. He didn't care.

He said he was worried by how cold it was because he hadn't got any money off the dole since he came out of prison 4 weeks before. I gave him all the cash I had in my wallet but the cashpoint in the hotel didn't work so I couldn't give him any more. He said it was OK, that I could transfer some money to his account.

At 1:30 am he left with a bottle of cider from the bar and £60 in his wallet.

He left me with an empty wallet and a feeling of being totally out of control again. He left me with that familiar misery that I have lived with for so long.

For the 3.5 hours he was with me I was like Sam out of Quantum Leap. I was back as the Dawn before I started seeing Trevor. In fact, I was the 18-year-old Dawn. It felt like almost everything I had didn't exist any more. The only reminder was the fact that I was sat in a bar in a hotel, having just given him a load of cash.

He left and I was shaken.

The next day I got up at 5am, having had a fitful sleep from 2am.

I made my way into college with my eyes to the ground and a maelstrom in my head. When I saw Trevor, the unfamiliarity was gone and there was the guy who had

Nothing Needs to be the Way it's Always Been

helped me find myself stood in front of me again. I wanted him to tell me it was OK, that I could cope. But I didn't want to tell him that I'd screwed up, met my brother and was now in this deep dark hole. After all, this was day 2 of the course – this was not about me.

So I stewed.

Every break I took myself off to a quiet space as soon as I could and I tried to work out what was going on in my head. I found myself distracted as we went through the day, wanting only to find a nice dark corner to sit in.

When the course finished I sent the others off on their own (I usually travel back to the airport with a couple of friends off the course). I slowly walked through Regents Park to Baker Street Tube. I chatted to the squirrels, observed the birds, watched my feet as they walked along.

I eventually settled in at the airport and started working on my exam pack for the course to try and get my head somewhere else. I gave in and emailed Trevor. He reassured me that I'd just stirred stuff up and it would settle.

It did start to settle. But it hasn't yet gone away.

I am still in the time warp.

I have realised a number of things.

I was stupid to think it was a good idea to meet with my brother.

I am not well enough established as the "new me" to cope with anything from my old life.

Dawn C. Walton

I can't help my brother.

I have a lot more work to do on myself.

I guess, like Sam from Quantum Leap, I need to take action on these feelings, then I can leap back to the me now. And get back to enjoying everything about my life. I think it's going to take a while longer for me to get back to enjoying being myself again.

Dawn C. Walton

22nd February, 2012

I'm back

You may not have realised I'd been away.

I've been posting every day as I usually do and sharing what goes on in my life with you all.

But I've been away in my head since I met my brother.

I'd lost my happy place and I just couldn't seem to find my way back.

It was weird because no matter what I tried, nothing seemed to make a difference. Not even Trevor's magic emails were making a dent in my misery.

Even the endorphins from a long run in the sunshine didn't help.

I was beginning to feel I'd lost my happy place for good. That everything that I'd achieved was superficial and had just collapsed with even the smallest nudge.

And yet…

…I knew this wasn't true. It's kind of hard to explain but there was no substance to the misery. It wasn't attached to an event, a memory, a thing. It was just a feeling.

My bounce was gone and I really didn't understand why.

Nothing Needs to be the Way it's Always Been

Then last night, as I once more reflected, I realised something.

I had shut down. I had gone back into the little safe protected spot in my head where I can't be hurt. It's been such a long time since I visited, I barely recognised it. It may be safe but it's no fun.

And now, I know what fun looks like and feels like. I know how good it is to feel happy and buoyant each day. I know how good it is to not be focussed inwards, protecting myself, but to be looking outwards and sharing with others.

So, having realised where I was, and why I was there, I made a decision.

I opened the door and stepped out.

And then I closed the door behind me.

And now I'm happy again. I'm back to having fun.

Phew!

23rd February, 2012 Dreams

I have always had bad dreams.

Most of the time I don't remember these dreams. Occasionally I do and they leave a shadow through the day.

Sometimes I don't dream much at all.

But what I know is when I remember dreams they are bad ones. With the same characters from my past in

Dawn C. Walton

them, and with the same generic theme of being out of control.

For the last two nights I've had good dreams.

Dreams that I felt good from when I woke up and I love it!

Even more interesting is the content of these 2 dreams.

The first one involved me doing a 5-mile run with a couple of friends from way back in the day (not the sort that would run). It was across fields and involved climbing on to the roofs of buildings – how bizarre! But I won the race and it was easy for me.

Then last night it was a weird sort of triathlon. I had to swim 4 lengths of a very short pool and then run up and down the edge of the pool 8 times. Tom Daley (the British diver) was there taking part. Again I won and again it was easy.

What weird dreams these are, eh? No idea what they mean but also, to some degree, don't care. Because they are good!

19th March, 2012

Getting to know me

Since I started seeing Trevor, the person I used to be has gradually diminished to be replaced by a new improved me.

It's taking some getting used to, to be honest. All those things that I thought I knew about myself have changed. Things I never expected to change have changed. Let me tell you a little bit about the new Dawn:

The new Dawn feels comfortable in new and unfamiliar situations. She is OK with going and asking someone where something is or how something works. Travel to new places is now viewed more as adventure than something that just needs a strategy for survival. She has become a bit too blasé when preparing for trips and now often forgets critical things in her new relaxed approach!

The new Dawn is comfortable with being seen as the expert on something. You can ask her for advice without her feeling guilty. She has always taken pleasure in helping others but tended to be self-absorbed and unwilling to accept it was a good quality of hers. Now she loves it. It's the best drug ever to do something to help someone else and to do it without guilt makes it even more potent.

Nothing Needs to be the Way it's Always Been

The new Dawn is able to see that the people around her love her and is able to at least acknowledge that she loves them. Displays of this affection remain more limited!

The new Dawn is comfortable in social situations. She finds herself striking up conversations with total strangers and gets pleasure in putting a smile on people's faces.

The new Dawn is comfortable with proximity and casual contact. When people touch her arm or shoulder, she no longer dives into a black box in her head to hide. The Tube in London is no longer a traumatic experience. As yet she is not comfortable with other forms of contact. She looks on jealously when people greet each other with a warm hug. The thought of seeing a physio for an injury has her physically shaking with fear at the thought. This type of contact is still scary.

The new Dawn spends a lot of time thinking about the future and how exciting it is. She makes plans for her life and how it will change. She has always believed anything is possible if you just believe, but this belief used to be based on "what have I got to lose?" and now it is based on "look how much I can gain".

The new Dawn is regarded as positive and chilled out. In the past, when people said this she would laugh and give herself a pat on the back for fooling them all. Now she is amused. Because this is not an act any more. This is really who she is.

The new Dawn knows what it is to feel happy. Indeed, what it is to feel everything. Emotions were always risky and so kept locked away. Now all emotions are available, which includes happiness. This continues to be a struggle as she struggles with how to cope and not become over-analytical on the bad days. But the good far outweighs the bad. She still has some way to go to accept that it's OK to be happy, though.

So this is me so far.

There is still more work to do, as you can see, but I have come a long way.

We are approaching a year since my first session with Trevor in the middle of June 2011. It took 39 years for me to become who I was. It has taken between 7 and 8 months to become who I now am.

That is pretty amazing, isn't it?

Things I have learnt.

1. When I'm tired I'm miserable. Our prefrontal cortex, which is responsible for rational thought, needs energy to function. When it is starved of energy we naturally resort to our emotional brain. This is why sleep-deprived parents struggle so much and why people struggling with depression get caught in a vicious cycle of insomnia and lows. It's a little unfamiliar to me this emotional stuff. As a result, I tend to feel very low when I'm tired. Those emotions don't tend to be the good ones and I feel exposed and vulnerable. I am still learning to not over-analyse those times and just wait for it to pass.

2. Nothing that used to be true is true any more. I can't, I won't, that's not who I am…all these things need

Nothing Needs to be the Way it's Always Been

to be challenged when they crop up. I need to ask myself "Really? Is that really true?" because maybe it isn't any more. I don't know me any more so I can't make judgements based on who I used to be. They are no longer valid.

3. My journey to this point in my life has given me all the resources I need to be able to help others in the best way I can. Cognitive Hypnotherapy has allowed me to unlock that potential. This is what I was meant to do. If nothing else, I am a better mother, partner and friend because of this.

4. I have some way still to go. I need to learn to forgive myself for my failings. I don't know how to do that right now. I desperately want to be comfortable with all forms of contact in the way I am now comfortable with so many other things. And above all, I want to tip the balance, into feeling like I am worthy of this happiness. Because I'm not quite there yet either.

This year the Dawn that will turn 40 in October is the new Dawn and I really can't wait

Dawn C. Walton

27th March, 2012

Feeling pathetic

This is a "feeling sorry for myself" post.

I need to write it out because one day I won't feel like this, but I do right now.

On the Quest forum (the one where the Cognitive Hypnotherapists go to discuss stuff) there has been a discussion thread about forgiveness.

And the gist has been, that to truly grow and move on from our protection state, then we need to learn to forgive those we feel wronged us, and also, the gold standard, forgive ourselves.

I've been thinking about this.

And I'm not ready.

Not ready to forgive anyone. Definitely not myself. I have no appetite for it. And I have to ask myself – what's that about? What do I gain from not letting go versus what I would gain from forgiveness?

Logically I know I should. Subconsciously I can't. And it's like a weight holding me back. Limiting me in so many ways.

Like right now.

Nothing Needs to be the Way it's Always Been

Last week, I had a twinge in my thigh before I went on my 3-hour run.

About 10 minutes into the run the muscle had warmed up and all was fine.

But when the muscle cooled down again it was way worse. It was no longer twingeing only when I ran but actually really painful when I walked. So much so, I am limping a little as I walk.

So I bought a heat pack, and some pain relief gel. I started stretching it out. I got some advice about a foam roller and bought one of those. So far it is stopping me exercising, which is OK but not ideal.

What I should do is go and get a sports massage or go and see a physio. Because that would sort it. It really is only a muscular thing. There are less than 4 weeks until I run the London Marathon and I need to look after myself for the big day.

But you see, I can't. I am too scared. The very thought of going to see someone, of having a massage, of that level of contact is terrifying for me. It is truly pathetic. There is nothing to be scared of.

Like with forgiveness, there is nothing to lose and everything to gain.

And yet I can't do it.

So right now I feel pathetic and useless and it's drowning out all my achievements. It's like they mean nothing because there is this one thing that I should be able to do but can't.

So yes, I'm feeling pretty down on myself right now.

And one day in the future, I will read this post and smile, because it will help me once more understand how far I've come in my journey.

But that day is a long way off…

Dawn C. Walton

18th April, 2012

I don't cry

In all the work Trevor and I have done in our sessions, one thing has never happened.

I haven't cried.

I don't, you see.

And it was one of the things that made me feel like a cold, heartless b***h. And to some degree I still feel that way but I am slowly warming up.

I am sure there was a time when I did cry. After all, all kids cry.

But some kids learn that there is no point. Because no one pays any attention if you do. Or maybe, because when you do you get shouted at and it just draws the worst sort of attention to you. A sort of attention you don't want.

When I was 6 or 7 I saved my crying until night time, with my head under my pillow. I learnt the art of silent crying where the tears flow but there is no sound. Other than the sound of the arguments, the fists through the door. The anger.

As I got older I learnt that I shouldn't cry. That it would give away my feelings, that it would make me vulnerable.

Nothing Needs to be the Way it's Always Been

I couldn't afford to be vulnerable. I had to be strong. To survive.

So I don't cry.

And these days, sometimes when the little one is telling me how she will be OK about certain things "if I fall over I won't cry mummy", or as I kiss her goodnight "I won't cry tonight, mummy" what do I say to her?

I tell her "It's OK to cry sometimes. Sometimes we need to cry because something hurts or we're upset. If you feel like crying, you go ahead and cry, darling" and I give her the biggest hug I can because sometimes, we just need to cry, don't we?

Dawn C. Walton

25th April, 2012

Virgin London Marathon 2012. Done...

I was neither nervous or excited as I waited in what was called a "pen" for the marathon to start. In fact, I felt the same as I'd felt all the way through this process – like it wasn't real. Because the idea of me running the London Marathon is so far beyond my ability to conceive.

Becca and Darin were in front of me. We'd met at Limehouse station and travelled with masses of runners to the red start.

Becca and Darin had completed their run prep like pros while I just stood around. The other runners who were sponsored by Nestle Pure Life had gathered for the PR photo and were discussing their estimated times. 3 hours. 4 hours. I said nothing. Increasingly I felt like I didn't belong here. I had only run for 3 hours and 13.5 miles.

My plan had been, finish the same day I start but then I read that if you didn't finish within 8 hours 15 minutes you didn't get a medal. I hoped for 5.5-6 hours.

But I felt like I didn't belong. I was just along for the ride. I was trusting in my training plan from Full

Nothing Needs to be the Way it's Always Been

Potential to have prepared me as I shuffled along behind Becca and Darin to the start.

And then we were running. They settled into their 9 minutes running, 1 minute walking routine. They'd done races together before. I tagged along behind. But my brain isn't used to stopping. I am used to a "keep going whatever" mentality and was finding 9+1 very tough. The problem was, at the time I didn't realise it was that. I just thought I was being crap. I thought that despite following my training plan religiously I wasn't well enough prepared for this.

Darin and Becca were soaking up the atmosphere and loving it. Darin was reaching out to high 5 all the kids with their arms out. He was like a true celebrity. People called out names from shirts. "Well done, Darin" they yelled. My rucksack was covering my name. Noone was yelling Dawn.

I tagged along.

Mile 3 came and it was the first Nestle Pure Life water stop. I decided to wait until mile 5 for the Lucozade. I'd been drinking the lite version in my training runs and liked the energy. But this was the full sugar and it was too sweet. It sat heavily on my stomach. After that I grabbed water every time there was a station and drank it before the next. I did well on keeping hydrated but my energy was low. Becca said she was having a gel so I had one. It also sat heavily in my stomach.

Darin kept veering off to shake hands. I tried to concentrate on keeping up. It wasn't working and so, at mile 6 I waved them on. I didn't want to hold them back.

Dawn C. Walton

After all, I didn't really belong there, doing that. It was their thing. I watched them disappear into the distance and felt useless.

I was only 6 miles in.

I had 20 to go and I was struggling.

But I'd done everything in my training plan. I'd run for 3 hours and this was 1 hour 15 ish. What was wrong with me?! I reached for my phone to look for the amazing support of my Twitter and Facebook friends. It was out of battery. I had a spare but needed it for the finish. I'd messed up my iPod at the start so had put that away.

If I was to finish this, for the next 20 miles I would be on my own.

I told myself I should be enjoying it. I should be getting a boost from the crowds. But I wasn't enjoying it and the crowds were doing nothing for me. I was still jogging. I switched to walking and occasionally jogging because I knew if I was to do this, the one thing I must not do is stop.

I ran the 26.2 miles without stopping a single time.

I tried to work out how I could quit. But couldn't find a way I could live with myself if I did. Besides, I couldn't let all of you down. With your encouragement and support and faith in me. All of you out there kept me going.

So I power walked and jogged. I started picking out fellow runners who were keeping pace with me. I went into pattern spotting mode!

Nothing Needs to be the Way it's Always Been

The guy with a full-size replica tiger on his back. He finished ahead of me. The crowd yelled "Oi, mate, you've got a tiger on your back" when he passed and he occasionally stopped to let the kids stroke it.

There was the overweight lady running on her own. Red-faced and struggling, she just kept on slowly jogging along.

Big Ben scooted off for a wee on the grass (he wouldn't have fitted in the Portaloos) and was followed by St. Pauls and the Gherkin.

The Oompa Lumpas, who were very tall, kept passing me and the audience always sang the tune as they passed.

If these people could do it, then I could.

As I reached halfway I was disappointed. My time was around 3 hours. The same as when I was training and walking up hills. I kept swapping between walking and running because it was easier to run - that's what my training prepared me for - but it was more exhausting. Every time I stopped to walk I found it harder.

I passed a few McDonald's and thought about going in for a Diet Coke and something to eat. Surely it must be lunchtime soon? I grabbed a Jelly Baby that someone was offering and it gave me a real energy boost. From then on I grabbed a Jelly Baby whenever it was offered. Luckily plenty of people lined the route with Jelly Babies! I kept looking at the crowd trying to get a lift from them. But I needed to just keep going.

Dawn C. Walton

Mile 14 was horrible. The course loops and overlaps with mile 22 on the other side. I had 3 more hours to go. They had about 25 minutes and were all running.

It was at around this point I passed Darin and Becca without realising it. They'd stopped for the loo.
I stopped for nothing. The one thing I would not allow myself to do was stop.

I couldn't afford to think about the end. I would get too desperate to finish. I had always said that if all else failed I would just walk it and when I was young I used to go on long walks with my grandmother so was comfortable in the belief that I could walk any distance. So I started pacing myself to about a 15-minute mile. It gave me something to focus on.

I wondered how far ahead of me Darin and Becca were.

I found the course quite boring and kept on reminding myself that I should be enjoying it. Getting a boost from the crowds. I wasn't. I didn't. I wondered why I was doing this but knew that now I had started, I would eventually finish and have that achievement.

3 miles before the end. I knew I'd finish now. I told myself that I easily ran 3 miles at home and started running more. The heavens opened. My Garmin watch ran out of batteries so I couldn't set a pace. It had been running about 3/4 mile ahead of the actual distance all along anyway. But it's nice to see the consistency in my splits when I downloaded the data.

Now I had no pace. 3 miles to go.

Nothing Needs to be the Way it's Always Been

I wondered if Becca and Darin were now getting dry. I wondered if there would be anyone to meet me. I'd seen noone along the route. I know Donna was somewhere around mile 3 but hadn't seen her.

I kept turning bends thinking it would be The Mall but it wasn't so I had to walk again. Eventually I was on the last straight. The crowds had mostly gone. I looked over at the Nestle Stand and it was empty. I raised my arms and smiled for the photo at the finish and finished the marathon in 6 hours 21 minutes. I got an official photo taken then grabbed a goody bag. I sat down on a dry bit of gravel, scoffed some fruit thing in the bag and swapped my battery to call my friend. We arranged to meet at the place where I was supposed to meet Darin and Becca.

I got there and there was noone around. So I sat down. I messaged Sandra, who I knew would be there for photos at the end. She asked where I was and where Becca and Darin were, which confused me! She headed over.

My friend and the little one came over and I gave the little one a big hug. She was soggy from standing in the rain. They had been on the other side of the road yelling at me, apparently.

I hadn't noticed.

Then Sandra appeared and then I saw Darin.

"You finished before us," he said.

I looked at him blankly.

240

Dawn C. Walton

He repeated it.

Apparently they'd stopped for the loo around mile 10 which is when I'd caught up and then at mile 16 he got a real problem with his calf that meant they had to walk. Sandra had missed me coming up to the finish but seen and photographed them.

We had a photograph with our medals (after someone had lifted me up!).

I hobbled off home. My injuries had been fine but 26.2 miles and 6 hours 21 minutes of running and walking meant my legs were totally knackered. Thanks to my anchor, my feet weren't tired though. This was just the muscles in my leg. Overnight on Sunday they got worse and they were agony on Monday but by Tuesday my legs were mostly recovered. So all good.

Just a few people I'd like to ~~blame~~ thank for running the marathon before I end this marathon post!

Thank you, Becca. If it wasn't for you, when Nestle Pure Life PR contacted me and asked if I would like to run the marathon I would have said no. Thank you for preparing so well and being so open in sharing that info and helping and guiding me. I know I am stubborn and I just couldn't seem to think my way through the logistics. Because of you I knew what to do when I finished the marathon on my own!

Thank you, Darin. You have been my inspiration to run more than one or two miles. I saw how you fought to build up your runs and how you succeeded in the Great South Run and then the Brighton half marathon.

Nothing Needs to be the Way it's Always Been

It inspired me to prove to myself that I could run those distances. Without that, I would never have said yes to running the marathon.

Thank you, Nestle Pure Life. You gave me a once in a lifetime offer that I couldn't say no to. You provided an excellent company in Full Potential, who write a training plan tailored to me and who were always there for advice. You kept in touch and sorted everything out for me. I feel very lucky to have been given this chance and am delighted that just before we set off we had raised at least £34k for the Samantha Dickson Brain Tumour Trust. I know we will raise more too.

Thank you to my friends on Twitter and Facebook. Your support kept me going before, during and after the race. You tracked me online, you donated to my charity, and you supported me constantly with messages. This is my Facebook stream after I posted my message

Just in case you weren't tracking me - I've just finished the London Marathon!

YAY Congrats! 35088 overall, 12080 by gender, 7137 by category. Place in my heart? No 1.;)

I hate the BBC btw - I was watching the (rain soaked) finish cameras - then just as you were due - they switched the flaming things over to snooker!!!!! AAAAARGGHH. Was sat there with camera and everything!

I was watching too, until they cut off at 4pm

Official time was 6.21.15 and it cut off at 6.20.00 grrrrrrrrrr

Dawn C. Walton

You were being tracked all 3 of you! well done! proud of you xxxxxxxx

Amazing achievement! Well done. Are you going to do another one:-D

I got knackered just looking at the tracker page!

And incidentally, Dawn says she's fine. Which is good to know as she had a knackered leg going into it!;)

Such an inspiration:) x

Naah, she'd doing anything to get out of cooking Sunday lunch;)

Fine! FINE! she's just run 26 and a bit miles - how can she be fine???!!!

Count legs - 2 - count working lungs - 2 - that's fine then!

I'm disappointed - no updates from you whilst running?;)

Seriously - WELL DONE! Just brilliant.

Count blisters - 27 - count aching muscles - all of them?

Also watching to hope to see you finish. Well done!!

count non-aching muscles may be better.;) Count level of urgency for a loo before coming over all Paula Radcliffe... hehe

Hehe:-D

Brilliant! Well done Dawn. Just the victory lap now:)

Amazing. You're a marathon runner! Couldn't believe it when they switched over to the snooker. We'd tracked you all the way and the boys were shouting 'come on'! Well done:)

Nothing Needs to be the Way it's Always Been

Well done! Xxx

<sniff> I knew you were running round with other men!;)

I was tracking you all afternoon...go you! Fantastic, inspirational, a massive well done x

You have done brilliantly I have been tracking you too!:-) Really well done

I'm waiting for Marathonfoto to come up with the pic at the finish...

YOU JUST RAN THE LONDON MARATHON!!!!!!! Gooo you!!! xx

Amazing well done!

Fanbloodytastic !!!!

Well done, Dawn - I was following your update page all day!!

Well done so impressive xx

Wow. Amazing!!!

Well done. An amazing achievement. X

Well done Dawn, so chuffed for you. Fantastic achievement. You're now a marathon runner for the rest of your life.:-) x

Soooo impressed Dawn!! WELL done, you're an inspiration! Hugs from Sweden!!

Congratulations Dawn!

I was also sat there with my camera (iPad) to take a photo when they bloody turned off, was furious!

Dawn C. Walton

Thanks all. Shame about the bbc but I will have a picture from my finish to share;)

Congratulations! What an amazing achievement! You must feel sore and cream crackered but fab!! xxx

What an amazing achievement. Well done just isn't sufficient to say! Ax

Well done Dawn - my sis finished too

Well done Dawn!!

Great effort! Well done. The world is definitely at your feet now! Big hugs from here

Lady - lady lady - so impressed! - so pleased for you, now get that dress on and go get that award!!! xxxxxxxxxxxxx

Thank you, Trevor. For helping me to see that life is for living. And for showing me that I have the most amazing people around me that I love to bits.

Thank you, Sandra. You and Thinking Slimmer started this whole journey off. I didn't just lose weight, but I found myself freakishly wanting to run where I never had before. And because you care so much that the Slimpod works for every single person, you picked up the phone to speak to me and changed my life with that one small action. I'm also happy and lucky enough to call you a friend these days.

Thank you, Hubby. Your unerring belief in me is amazing. And despite the disruption the marathon training caused to our lives you never for one minute complained or made me feel bad about doing it. Your faith and pride in me since the moment we got together

Nothing Needs to be the Way it's Always Been

has allowed me to become anything I want to be. Your message on Facebook on the day of the marathon was amazing:

I can't begin to say how impressed I am with Dawn. She's taken on this marathon and given it everything. All through the winter she's kept up her training, even the bit she hates (intervals), using the treadmill when it was too horrible to go outside. This is while doing her main job, her second job (the hypnotherapy), spending time with the little one, and, most importantly, going for takeways. You're incredible Dawn. Nice butt too.;)

I love you more than the world and am so lucky to have you as my hubby.

Dawn, marathon runner, 6 hours 21 minutes.

Am I glad I did it? Yes.

Did I enjoy it? No.

Would I do it again? Never.

Dawn C. Walton

30th April, 2012

Living in an alternate reality

There is some imposter living my life right now.

I don't know who she is but she's having a great time.

How dare she steal my life and have more fun with it than me!

This woman has come into my life and chosen to live it very differently. She trained for and ran the London Marathon in my body – something that only 1% of the population achieve in their lifetimes. The cheek of it!

She is training to be a Cognitive Hypnotherapist, has set up a website and is in the process of converting my garage so she can set up in business. She has been successfully helping many people along the way as she completes her training.

This woman has found a happiness and appreciation of my life in a way that I have struggled so much to do.

At first I was pretty miffed at the woman. How dare she!

Then I was jealous of what she was able to do with the same life and same resources as I have.

Now I am in awe of what she has achieved. I am watching her and trying to learn from her.

Because one day I hope that I can be her.

Dawn C. Walton

6th May, 2012

My sister

I have a sister. She has 2 kids. The little girl is about 6 months younger than the little one – the little boy a couple of years younger.

I don't talk about her much. To be honest, we are still getting to know each other. Both the hubby and I have a lot of respect for her. She has had a very tough few years. Her pregnancies have not been easy and her relationship with their father even worse. We don't know much about it because she deals with it on her own with lots of strength. Even if I did, it wouldn't be for me to share.

Let me tell you why we are just getting to know each other.

She is the daughter of my stepmother and my father.

She was born shortly before my brother and I left to live with my mother and stepfather. She was still a baby when we left home so we knew about her but she never knew about us.

When I went to live with my mother, my father wanted nothing more to do with me. Obviously my stepmother didn't as she hated us.

Nothing Needs to be the Way it's Always Been

I believe my sister only found out she had a brother and sister when she was around 16 and a school friend asked after us. We'd all gone to the same primary school, you see.

She went home and asked my father and he confirmed it was the truth. So she was brought up as an only child. She had a very different life to me. It was a happy, well cared for family life. When she was 18 she wrote to me and I immediately wrote back. I met with her not long after.

At that stage her parents had split and she'd been left to fend for herself – having to find somewhere to live and a job to support herself. This was a bit of a shock for her.

It was really difficult for me.

How do you reconcile why you are unlovable but your sister isn't? How do you not make that about you? Same parents, completely different childhood. We were starved, hit and lived in fear every day. She was fed well, not hit and even had family holidays.

For many years I searched for answers. What is it about me? My brother would visit my father in later years when we moved to a house only 2 miles away. They would chat. When I tried to visit I was sent away with my tail between my legs. What was it about me? How bad must I be that even as a child I was so difficult to love?

But after seeing Trevor I don't need answers any more. I am OK with that all now. That in itself is pretty amazing. And it makes my relationship with my sister a lot easier.

Dawn C. Walton

I know it has been hard for her. I have shared with her what happened in my childhood, with both sets of parents. I have also made it clear that she has no responsibility in the process, because she doesn't.

My brother and I are both in touch with her these days. I wish I lived closer because I would love to help her out more and I would also love the little one to have a relationship with her cousins. Ironically, my stepmother and mother now live in the same village. It's still hard to feel any sort of real connection with my sister but we both work at the relationship and she knows I will always be here for her and the kids. She's been going it alone for many years now, and doing a great job.

So I don't talk about her on here much because we don't have a huge amount of contact but I do occasionally mention her and wanted to share a little bit of our story.

Dawn C. Walton

9th May, 2012

Not quite there...

This weekend it is weekend 8 of 10 of my Cognitive Hypnotherapy course and I've changed my flights to travel down earlier on Friday so that I can have a session with Trevor.

In June it will be a year since I had that first session. We have now had 4 sessions and you'll have seen from previous posts how much has changed.

And that's how I know there are still things we need to work on.

Let me put this in perspective for you. I am probably one of the few people in the world who can run the London Marathon as the first ever time running in an organised race – and, in fact, running with other people around – and feel disappointed in herself. Even I know there is something wrong with not being able to see the achievement in that!

During the training, I needed physiotherapy on an injury. And I couldn't make myself go and get some. It just sent me into a panic at the thought of it. So clearly, whilst I am so much more comfortable in myself and around others, there is still something that needs sorting here.

Nothing Needs to be the Way it's Always Been

And finally, and probably linked to all of the above, I know I have an emotional block around food that I can't get rid of on my own. I want to continue losing weight on Thinking Slimmer and I have reached a point where my refusal to change what I eat is getting in the way of progress.

At first I was quite excited at the prospect of being able to make another leap and see how different I would be after. I am particularly looking forward to having a beer or few with Sandra and Becca on Friday evening and celebrating running the marathon. But as we get closer, I get more nervous (as usual) because I know now what I have to do to make this change. And I know it's not easy and requires a lot from me, under Trevor's guidance.

So it's another big week for my head and this personal journey I'm on. But it's worth it. My life is amazing these days.

6 - Session 5

Dawn C. Walton

13th May, 2012

Deep in thought

I know I've been a bit quiet. I will write a post about my weekend in more detail later in the week.

But for now I went to see Trevor for a session on Friday. I didn't think I'd need any more sessions, to be honest. I've had 4 since June last year and I've changed so much. Increasingly I have leant on him less and less. I used to mail him all the time to keep me on track. I haven't done that for a couple of months now.

It's interesting. People have expressed concerns about a dependency on Trevor but a good few years ago, when I saw a person-centred counsellor almost every week for well over a year, no one expressed concerns about dependency then...

But anyway, it's because I have come so far that I knew I needed to see him again. Because I am so happy with my life now and what I do with it. People have noticed how much more comfortable I seem in my own skin. How much more positive I am. And it's all true. So much has changed that I am barely recognisable to myself...

...and yet.

And yet whilst I am happy enough with what I do, I have continued to hate who I am. I have a voice in my head

Nothing Needs to be the Way it's Always Been

swearing at me and criticising me all the time. And it was time to get rid of that. That's why I went to see Trevor. Because it doesn't belong with the new version of me but rather than disappearing, it's been getting worse.

Trevor talks about the steps he hopes to take a client through. They start off believing in him, then in both of us, and finally in themselves. As therapists it is our goal to get the client to the self-belief stage so they don't need us any more.

I liken it to jumping a chasm.

At first Trevor takes my hand and we go and look at the chasm, and talk about what is on the other side (the solution state). This is belief in him.

Then we hold hands and run. He shows me the right pace to run at to have enough momentum to jump and in that run-up I begin to believe I can do it. This is belief in both of us.

Then, at just the right moment when I say it's OK, he lets go of my hand and I take the leap. This is belief in myself.

Not all clients will go through all these stages and not all clients will get to the last stage. But this is the goal.

I wanted to leap the chasm but I still didn't know how.

Because I don't believe in myself. I hate myself. Despite all my achievements.

So we talked. And we explored my Subconscious. We tried to find what was causing it. We found the place but

Dawn C. Walton

I didn't know where it was and what it was all about. But I knew that if, in that place, I could forgive myself, then I could leap that chasm and find true happiness.

That leap didn't happen during the session. Because that is down to me. But I know what I need to do, I just don't know if I can do it - no matter how much I want to...

As I processed that session later in the day, some things became clear to me and I emailed Trevor to let him know. As ever, he responded in a way that helped me shift my thinking again. Just a fraction.

There is all-out war going on in my head right now. That part of me that wants to leap the chasm and reach that true happiness on the other side, fighting the part of me that I hate so much. So the weekend has been challenging, not because of the course content, but because of the battle going on in my head. I have felt minutes away from meltdown. I have been physically shaking with the exertion of pushing against that resistance to accept that I am anything but useless and crap. At times I have felt the tears trying to escape.

But as I left the course this afternoon, I joined the other people on the course in giving Trevor a goodbye hug. And you know what? That was fine. I was fine. So something has already changed. I'm sure other changes will follow. In time. I will leap that chasm and whilst Trevor is no longer holding my hand, I do know he is there ready to catch me if I need it, and encouraging and cheering me on if I don't.

Nothing **Needs to be the Way it's Always Been**

At this rate, by the time we are a year on from that first session in mid-June last year, I will have found true happiness in all dimensions of my life. You have to admit, that is pretty stunning by any standards, isn't it?

Dawn C. Walton

15th May, 2012

The Gallery - Born to Run

Did that make you giggle? Not what you might associate with me, is it? It's the title of a brilliant book by Chris McDougall that has inspired me back to running.

Yesterday morning I threw on my tracksuit bottoms, grabbed a T-shirt from the cupboard and donned my sports bra. These days, that sports bra is the only thing I wear that is "running gear". Since the marathon I have gone back to running in my scruffy clothes.

My Garmin Forerunner watch had run out of charge. So I grabbed my iPod, set up the Nike+ for 20 minutes of running and shuffle on songs and headed out for a run.

It was sunny and windy. There were puddles everywhere from all the rain over the last few days.

My head was full of thoughts that I needed to work through.

This is why I started running.

Just under a year ago I had my first Cognitive Hypnotherapy session with Trevor Silvester. It changed a lot. One of the big things that happened is that it unlocked my emotions. Something that I had always seen as dangerous – I had them locked safely away.

Nothing Needs to be the Way it's Always Been

As a result, as well as being able to feel true happiness for the first time, I was also increasingly moody, miserable and snappy.

I had a real problem with that. It was not how I saw myself. I spoke to Trevor about it and he suggested I take up yoga or even just go for a walk each day.

I am very lucky in that I live by a disused railway line. So I stepped out of the house the next morning and went for a walk. I had put on my trainers because I figured if I was out anyway, then I may as well try and run a bit to get some exercise and help with weight loss. Noone would see me because we live in the middle of nowhere.

I walked and jogged a little. After seconds I was red-faced and panting so I walked again. I walked to the end of the first bit of path and then back. Jogging for seconds at a time. I think that first outing took me about 28 minutes to do 1.2 miles.

But I turned it into a habit. Each day I put on my "running gear" when I got up instead of my clothes for the day. I didn't make it a choice. Irrespective of the weather I went for a walk/run. Gradually increasing the running instead of walking. Eventually I tried for a longer run one day a week...getting up to 2 miles and thinking that might be the furthest I would ever manage.

I made it a habit because I hated it. But you see, running is one of the few things you can't find an excuse not to do. It's right outside my door. I don't need equipment. I just run.

Dawn C. Walton

And things changed. My moods changed. I started the day positive and light with a sense of achievement. I found the endorphins I was getting from running carried me through the whole day and I lost my 2pm slump where all I wanted to do was sleep. I was no longer permanently tired – even if the little one had a terrible night.

Running was addictive.

And it was that path that led me to the marathon. But it was also that path that took away this feeling I was getting from running. Because I started running for a purpose. I had to run a certain way, a certain distance to train. I was no longer doing it to clear my head and I didn't like that.

Marathon over. I've proved I can do that distance. There is nothing left to prove.

So yesterday morning I stepped out of my front door to clear my head. To get the endorphins to carry me through the day.

One foot in front of the other. As I set off feeling that usual doubt about how I can keep going. Running isn't easy for me. It never has been and I suspect it never will be.

Up the small hill onto the path. I can see now the blue sky with the clouds. I can see the wind swaying the trees. A rabbit crosses my path as I recover my breath from the hill and find my pace on the uneven surface. On some mornings I would have no way of knowing how beautiful the sunrise was unless I went for a run.

Nothing Needs to be the Way it's Always Been

"Just jog," I tell myself. "There is no hurry, just enjoy it."

I start to process everything in my head and soon forget how my body feels. I enjoy keeping my body occupied while my head does its job. Moments of insight flow in and out of my head and I occasionally notice what's going on around me.

I struggle to breathe. I have started my return leg and the wind is blowing on my face. My heart is racing from my thoughts. I push on, focussing more internally.

I occasionally wonder if my foot is going to start hurting but it doesn't.

1/2 a mile to go. I stop to walk. The wind is too much. I am cross with myself and then I realise it doesn't matter. I am just out to clear my head. That thought allows me to start running again.

I round the corner to my house and sprint to get that last boost.

I feel that sense of achievement of having had a run again. Things have made more sense and I start my day knowing I will have all the energy I need to get through it. All the energy I need to have the mood I choose.

This is why I run.

Dawn C. Walton

18th May, 2012

If I can do what I love I can love who I am

A fellow Cognitive Hypnotherapist, Chloe, wrote a blog recently about a big black cloud – and she ended with this phrase (which has different flavours by the way!):

"It's better to light a candle than curse the darkness."

This phrase talks to me right now.

It's a week today since I had session number 5 with Trevor and I have found myself wondering why I do this to myself? Why don't I accept the way things are? I was happy with my life. I was looking forward to my future. Everything was good in a way it had never been before.

But I still went for a Cognitive Hypnotherapy session with Trevor. Why is that?

It was because, despite all these things, I was not happy with me. For some reason I was unable to make my achievements about me. They were something I did, not who I was.

And that was enough to allow me to continue to wallow in my misery. Something I have become quite a pro at over the years!

Nothing Needs to be the Way it's Always Been

But it seems, despite believing I'm not a very positive person, I can't help striving to make things better. When given the choice, it seems I choose to light the candle (and curse the darkness at the same time).

I've had some pretty challenging sessions so far and this was up there as one of the hardest. Maybe because this is the last big thing I need to overcome. For quite a number of days afterwards I felt like at any moment I was just going to go into meltdown.

How does it feel? Well, think about a jar filled with water with silt at the bottom. Now pick that jar up and give it a good old shake. That's how I've been feeling all week.

But the silt is starting to settle. The good thing is that I am used to looking for positive changes now. I used to blog it in the early days and this is why these posts are tagged "positive of the day".

This is a tough one, though, because what I am aiming for is a change in attitude. I needed to change from "I am happy with my life" to "I am happy being me" and that has caused all-out war in my head!

It's hard to find signs that things have changed. Especially when some of the signs seem to be things I don't want. For a few days after the session I didn't want to eat. The first thing to shut down when I am in turmoil or very upset is my appetite. By Tuesday that had passed and since then I have been eating anything and everything I can lay my hands on. I feel like I am constantly scoffing and that scares the heck out of me! Now, I expected a change in my behaviour around food after the session. I am aware that beyond the

Dawn C. Walton

help the Slimpods have given me, I have an emotional attachment to food. I hoped, and am still hoping, that this work will overcome that. But right now it's going the wrong way!

Then on Wednesday I had an awful day. I just wanted to cry all day. I am aware that I am clinging on to something and I don't know why. I am resisting this change. And it's making me mad at myself. Honestly, do I really want to see myself as useless and pathetic? Why would I hold on to that view when I have been given a way to change it?

I went to my friends on Twitter and asked them if there was anything I could help anyone with. Because being able to use what I have learnt, both from my past and from the Cognitive Hypnotherapy course, allows me to see the point in all of this. And then the next day I got an amazing mail from someone who has used my chronic pain download. It has worked so well they've been able to stop taking their pain meds.

I went from rock bottom to cloud 9 in the space of a few words.

And that is when I realised that the path to liking myself is laid out before me. I am already walking it. Doing what I love, using my experiences and my skills to help other people, is what will allow me to become the person I love.

And with Trevor's help, I am gradually learning to accept my achievements as being about who I am and not just what I do.

Nothing Needs to be the Way it's Always Been

So this is where I am 1 week on. In the smallest of ways I am beginning to forgive myself. And from that I can begin to accept who I am and not just what I do.

One day soon I will be telling you how happy I am with my life and how happy I am being me.

Dawn C. Walton

22ⁿᵈ May, 2012

Ha! I ran the marathon

I know, I know, this is old news isn't it?

But you see, I haven't been able to acknowledge it. All I could see was how I failed. I didn't run for enough of it. I didn't have enough energy because I didn't have the right breakfast.

All the things I knew I should have done, I hadn't.

So completing the marathon gave me no sense of achievement. No buzz. I felt as flat at the end as I had at the start.

In the last 2 weeks I've been able to get back to my morning run before I start work. This is the run that I started to clear my head. This is the run that I did to give me energy to get through my day. I need this run.

So yesterday morning, as I ran along the path on my 2 mile route, I was thinking.

I thought "This is not easy".

I thought "I should be finding this a lot easier, shouldn't I? I ran 26.2 miles after all."

And then I realised.

Running is not easy for me.

Nothing Needs to be the Way it's Always Been

6 hours and 21 minutes was a great achievement for someone like me who doesn't even like running and struggles to run 2 miles!

I was being way too hard on myself – beating myself up for not running more of the 26.2 miles – but I struggle to run 2.

26.2 miles was an amazing achievement for me.

And now I know I can do it. I have nothing left to prove.

As I struggled along on my 2-mile route, I realised that just doing this regularly was an achievement. Getting out and running when I find it so hard is an achievement.

Running a marathon – no matter how long it took – is an achievement when you don't even enjoy running.

And so now I think I can have a beer and celebrate the fact that I ran the London Marathon this year…and I never have to run a race again. 2 miles a day is fine.

7 – The Beginning

Dawn C. Walton

24th May, 2012

I forgive you

This is a letter from the adult me to the child me.

Dear Dawn,

It must have seemed like a pretty tough break all these years. Having gone through your formative years having to fight for survival after being dealt a pretty poor deck of cards on the family front, you then had to take a barrage of abuse and hatred from me.

I'm sorry for that.

I was confused. I blamed you. I blamed you for doing whatever you needed to do to survive until you could get out on your own and control your own life. I misinterpreted your approach as weak and pathetic where I can see now you were strong and determined.

There were moments too where you were hugely brave. Despite the fear you had and the dependency of being a child, you stood up for yourself countless times in ways where even once would have been a massive achievement. I can think of three or four times where you did something amazing to stand up for yourself (that kick that broke his ribs will always make me smile). It wasn't your fault that it made no difference to your circumstances. I can see that now.

Nothing Needs to be the Way it's Always Been

It worked, though, because you survived and you have this amazing life with the most amazing people in it. That is because of who you are.

I'm sorry I blamed you. I was hurting. It seemed so unfair. Everything I did felt like a "despite..." not a "because of..." and I was always looking for answers. I see now that there were no answers. Sometimes shit happens. Sometimes shit happens lots.

I think we have both struggled to see that this wasn't about us.

I have blamed you. I thought you pathetic and useless. I felt you held me back because no matter what I achieved in my adult life, I felt you had let me down when I was a child. I was wrong.

It's because of you that I am who I am. I am strong and determined. I respect people irrespective of who they are or where they've come from. And now I am doing the most amazing thing because I am using everything we've been through to help other people. Without you, that wouldn't be possible.

So I'm sorry. But I don't forgive you, because I realise now there is nothing to forgive.

Instead I want to thank you. Thank you for looking after me and for getting me to where I am now.

Dawn C. Walton

27ᵗʰ May, 2012

What forgiveness means

Following on from my "I forgive you" post I wanted to give you some more on what led me to that point and what it means in my day-to-day life.

Children up until the age of 10 or so, tend to have limited processing skills. If they thought about running a race they might understand that they came first or second, they might even understand that they nearly won if they are a little older but they wouldn't understand all the shades of grey around the effort they put in, how the others in the race performed, the conditions etc. And it is with that limited thinking that memories are stored in our subconscious for use as a foundation for everything we do in later life.

As we become adults we gain the ability to process our thoughts in a multi-dimensional way with all those different shades of colour. Now, when we look back on those childhood memories, it is with the deeper understanding rather than the understanding that was used by the child at the time.

I guess you can see how that can end up with a disconnect? I view events from my childhood and try to understand them with my adult perspective and it is a hugely inaccurate way to do it.

Nothing Needs to be the Way it's Always Been

Also you know that term "hindsight is a wonderful thing"? Well, what makes hindsight so powerful is the whole concept of "if I knew then what I know now". So at any given point, we make the best choices we can with the information available based on our circumstances. Obviously, when we can see consequences, we have more information but we don't know that at the time. This is why I don't believe in regrets.

And as we get older we can't remember everything so we tend to forget what we feel is insignificant (forget consciously not subconsciously) and accentuate what we feel is significant.

So for me, coming to the realisation that all those events throughout my childhood were responded to in the best way I knew how to at the time, given my circumstances and the ability I had as a child, allowed me to leap that chasm. To believe in myself because I accepted I did the best I could at the time. And with this new insight I could also see all those occasions where I really did something unusually brave given my circumstances.

And for the first time in my life I have stopped beating myself up. I have allowed myself to accept my achievements. Before I hated myself so much that I refused to accept that anything good I did was because of a good quality in me. Now I can accept that I have done great things that I can be proud of.

So do I bounce out of bed every day and sing songs to the birds like a Disney princess? Not at all!

Dawn C. Walton

I have shadows. A lifetime of self-loathing and misery doesn't disappear that easily. But I have an answer to that critical voice now if it does crop up. I don't need to listen to it any more.

I also feel a huge sense of freedom. I am unburdened by the need to caveat everything that happens with "ah, but you're crap".

Unfortunately that sense of freedom also applies to food. My emotional connection to it has gone and now all I want to do is eat! I am trusting in my Slimpod right now in the hope it will kick in better control again soon.

I am getting to know myself from scratch. I am learning how to interact with the world all over again. It's interesting!

2nd June, 2012

Let me introduce you...

…to the new me.

I am now who I always have been but never realised it. I am a strong and determined person who has a great sense of fun. I love people and I love my life. Most of all I love the hubby and the little one. And these days I have fun with all of that. I enjoy who I am and what I do.

This is the Dawn I was always supposed to be.

Let me take you on my journey.

The room is bare. The walls are grey and there are no curtains but the windows are so dirty that there is very little light coming into the room. It's not quiet, though. There are muffled sounds coming from outside of the room. A sign of a world out there. Of lives being lived. Occasionally there is laughter.

I am in the corner of this room. Trying to make myself as small as I possibly can so as not to be noticed. I am wearing a nightie and am sat with my knees up to my chest with my nightie over them and my arms wrapped around them.

My head is down and I am sobbing.

Nothing Needs to be the Way it's Always Been

I am hiding. But it's not working because I can't hide from what's inside my head. And that's why I'm sad. I am tired of trying and I just want to disappear.

I can hear the world carrying on around me and I really want to be part of it. I'm jealous when I hear the laughter. But I'm too scared.

Then one day a man comes into the room. He sits down next to me. He talks to me. He shows me what the stuff in my head means. He helps me understand that it's not my choice it's there. He helps me get rid of it. Then he leaves the room and I think about what I've learnt.

The next day, when he comes in I'm no longer crying and I am staring out of the dirty windows. I even manage to smile at him. He walks over to the windows and cleans them to let the light in. It's a bit of a shock and I'm too scared to look out of them yet but we chat some more. He helps me understand that I can look out of the windows, that those demons in my head don't have control over me.

The next day when he comes I am stood up looking out of the window. There are great things to see out there and it is giving me pleasure to watch them. I smile at him as he walks in. He joins me as we look out of the window. We chat and he gets me thinking about what it might be like to be part of the world outside the window. When he leaves I watch him. Noticing for the first time the door that he has walked in and out of. He stops at the door to wave. To reinforce that option.

It's a couple of days before he comes again. By the time he does I have tried opening that door. I have started

Dawn C. Walton

to think about stepping out but am not brave enough. He takes my hand and we walk through the door together. There are so many people and things outside. It's amazing. I'm excited and he shows me that I am part of this world. That it's been my choice to stay in the room. This time when he leaves I stay outside of the room.

I enjoy this world. I realise how much I have missed. I talk to people and visit other rooms and really enjoy it.

But there's still something. I keep going back to my room because I don't feel like I should be part of this. I feel like an imposter. Because I still hate myself.

One day, as I explore I come across the man in one of the rooms. And we chat. And he teaches me that there was no reason for me to be in that room in the first place. It was not my fault that I was there. He shows me that I have a choice. I have walked through the door and now I can do anything I want. This time I walk out and run and sing and have fun and feel no need to go and find the man again.

I know he'll always be there if I need him anyway.

And that's where I am.

I have my own thoughts back in my head and they are such happy buoyant thoughts it's just brilliant. I didn't know this is what it would be like. I had no idea what the world would be like for me without those demons.

I feel connected to people and everything in a way I didn't know was possible. Without the "back off,

Nothing Needs to be the Way it's Always Been

buddy" shield, there is no resistance and people, contact, openness - nothing is scary any more.

I am planning my 40th birthday in October. I want a big party with all my friends there and I'm so excited. Before, I would have hated the thought of that

I am me. Unconstrained by defence mechanisms. No longer kept in my place mentally by a voice that hates me.

I am free to be whoever I want to be. And that is *so much fun.*

Less than 1 year after my first Cognitive Hypnotherapy session with Trevor I've moved from a curled-up ball of a person who was scared of the world and hated herself to a person who is stood on top of a hill with her arms spread, free and laughing like Maria from the Sound Of Music (without the singing - don't panic).

Now when the little one asks "Are you happy, mummy?" then I answer:

"YES!"

This is the beginning of my life. I can't believe it's taken me 40 years to get here but I fully intend to make the most of it from this point forward!

Appendix - A comment from the hubby

Dawn C. Walton

Dawn really has gone through incredible changes over the last year and a half. The problem is, when she's on a high she's enjoying herself, not blogging about it, so this account misses some real highs.

The most important one for me is how much she has helped other people. Confidentiality has stopped her blogging about this but in practising (unpaid) what she has learned she has: removed pregnancy stress from an expectant mother with a history of miscarriages; removed pain from a number of people (including one person who is firmly convinced she is a witch), chronic pain sufferers who've been able to reduce, stop, pain medication; remove my life-long fear of heights.

She is good at this. When she helps somebody, she is absolutely buzzing.

This has led to another change as well. She actually talks to people. Admittedly, she can be a pain in the butt with her evangelical little 'I can fix that' statements, like the Bob the builder of Cognitive Hypnotherapy. The fact is, though, she usually can. Dawn has always got her buzz out of being good, really good, at what she does. This is feeding that happy buzz.

That doesn't mean everything is rosy in the garden. Her step-parents are still crap and what they did to her as a child makes me want to reach for a shotgun. What happened is never going

Nothing Needs to be the Way it's Always Been

to change. How she deals with it already has done. Crap things still happen, as they do for everyone, at work, at home. She deals with it differently now, though.

She's missed things out about work. Her status and stature at work have improved enormously because, rather than staying in the background doing genius work, she's out there in people's faces now. The day after running the marathon she drove up to Blackpool to receive an award for some excellent work done by her people at an industry ceremony.

And she's changed with the little one. She's engaged with her more rather than seeing her as an extra chore in the day. That is a hugely unfair statement but at times it has been justified. She is a great mother and always has been but there have been times when she's not been left with much to give to others. She's got her sense of humour back, she's got seriously into baking, she's had more fun.

So she has changed. A lot. And that scares the hell out of me. Because I'd got used to coping with depressed Dawn. I knew the tricks to divert her worst moods, what buttons to push to distract her. Even at university me and some other friends used to tease her, saying (in a funereal voice) "my life is a dim, dark cellar. Oh joy" when her mood was on her. So it went back a long way. She was fun, though, when she wasn't down; caring, despite her protestations of not 'doing' emotion; and interesting, always, always interesting.

So now I have to relearn Dawn. Without an idiot's guide. So it's scary, for both of us as she's in the same position learning about herself. Ah well, we always liked a challenge. Bring it on.

About the author:

Dawn was born in Wales in 1972 and has lived in the UK her whole life. She has travelled the world extensively with work but now lives in Scotland where she has her Cognitive Hypnotherapy practice to help others in the same way that she has been helped.

Connect with Me Online:
Twitter: http://twitter.com/the_moiderer
My blog: http://www.themoiderer.com
My Cognitive Hypnotherapy website:
http://www.thinkitchangeit.com

Printed in Great Britain
by Amazon.co.uk, Ltd.,
Marston Gate.